GUARANTEED ANNUAL INCOME

THE MORAL ISSUES

GUARANTEED ANNUAL INCOME

THE MORAL ISSUES

Philip Wogaman

ABINGDON PRESS

NASHVILLE AND NEW YORK

GUARANTEED ANNUAL INCOME: THE MORAL ISSUES

Copyright © 1968 by Abingdon Press

Library of Congress Catalog Card Number: 68-27626

Scripture quotations unless otherwise noted are from the Revised Standard Version of the Bible, copyrighted 1946 and 1952 by the Division of Christian Education, National Council of Churches, and are used by permission.

Quotations from *Choruses from "The Rock"* by T. S. Eliot are from *Collected Poems 1909-1962*, copyright © 1934 by Harcourt, Brace & World, Inc. and by Faber & Faber, Ltd., and are reprinted by permission of the publishers.

Quotations from "Guaranteed Annual Incomes" by Leon H. Keyserling are reprinted by permission of *The New Republic*, © 1967, Harrison-Blaine of New Jersey, Inc.

Quotations from a May 2, 1966, advertisement in *Newsweek* are reprinted by permission of The Warner & Swasey Company.

SET UP, PRINTED, AND BOUND BY THE
PARTHENON PRESS, AT NASHVILLE,
TENNESSEE, UNITED STATES OF AMERICA

dedicated to my father

DONALD FORD WOGAMAN

who in his life and ministry
embodied a warm compassion for
the poor and an openness to
new economic ideas

ACKNOWLEDGMENTS

While accepting full responsibility for the contents of this book, I wish to thank several people who have improved it by reading and criticizing the manuscript. This assistance has been rendered by Luther E. Tyson and Leonard Boche of the Methodist Board of Christian Social Concerns and by my colleagues L. Harold DeWolf, James C. Logan, and Haskell M. Miller of the Wesley Theological Seminary, Washington, D. C. For two years, Dean DeWolf, Dr. Miller, and I have jointly taught a basic course on Christian Ethics and the Social Order, and I know that the book has also benefited in many unconscious as well as conscious ways from our conversations on problems in economic ethics.

I also wish to thank a study group at the Hughes Methodist Church of Wheaton, Maryland, for thoughtful consideration of the manuscript over a period of weeks. The men and women of this group were helpful critics. Moreover, their mature discussions encourage me to believe that even the most controversial questions in economic ethics can be approached in a deep and serious way by those who are not specialists.

Finally, I am grateful to my wife for her encouragement and patience and for her excellent criticism of both the style and content of the book, and I am grateful to our children for their patience when it was necessary for their father to absent himself behind the closed study door.

PHILIP WOGAMAN

CONTENTS

INTRODUCTION

In November, 1966, several hundred businessmen came to Washington, D. C., for a significant conference sponsored by the United States Chamber of Commerce. The purpose of this event was to provide an airing of the current proposals for a national "guaranteed annual income" or "negative income tax." Robert Theobald, Milton Friedman, and James Tobin were on hand to present papers in support of this or that form of income guarantee. Henry Hazlitt was present to denounce every such scheme, and Congressman Thomas Curtis spoke in support of what he called "guaranteed opportunity for all."

It was, in some respects, remarkable that the U. S. Chamber of Commerce should sponsor such an event. The Chamber, which has not in the past been noted for its support of new social welfare programs, was here providing a platform for the most "far-out" social welfare idea of all: the notion that in one way or another the government ought simply to *give* the poor a minimum income and have done with the more parsimonious haggling over means tests, questions of earning and deserving, the matter of legitimacy of children, or other spiritual heritages of the Elizabethan poor laws. The Chamber was not, of course, itself supporting the new concept. It was impeccably objective and fair in its presentation of the pros and cons. Moreover, its motivation in sponsoring the conference may have been partly to alert the business community to a concept which many people erroneously believed Congress would be debating vigorously in 1967. But

13

the truly remarkable thing about this national gathering (and its sponsorship) is that it indicated so clearly that the concept of guaranteed income cannot any longer be considered utopian nonsense. Some may consider it unwise or immoral. But it cannot any longer be dismissed as impractical—either economically or politically.

This point is underscored by the fact that Milton Friedman made one of the main addresses in support of an income guarantee. Friedman is one of the most highly respected conservative economists in the nation. In 1964 he was one of Senator Goldwater's main economic advisers, a fact which may help to identify him ideologically. As we shall note, he defends the "negative income tax" approach on grounds of efficiency, economy, and humaneness to the poor. Recognizing that no civilized country can allow people to starve to death (a point with which most conservatives and liberals are in agreement), Friedman believes that a flat minimum income grant to the impoverished could make it possible to dispense with the whole welfare apparatus, thus saving enormous sums. He argues, moreover, that such an approach would more effectively safeguard the freedom of the welfare recipient. Certainly any new social proposal which commands the interest of conservative economists such as Friedman, along with the enthusiastic support of more liberal thinkers such as Robert Theobald and Leon Keyserling, must be taken seriously by everybody.

But the *really* striking thing about the Chamber's national conference was that everybody's viewpoint, in the final analysis, hinged upon ethical issues. Granted the economic and political possibility (concerning which more will be said later), is it *moral* for people to be given income which they have not earned and may not deserve? This, we may suppose, is where the real debate will lie as Americans explore the deeper ramifications of guaranteed income.

A word of warning and of reassurance may be in order. Efforts are sometimes made in great national debates over public policy to suggest that questions involving economics or politics are too technical and complicated for the untrained layman to grasp. It is true that complex technical questions cannot be oversimplified

14

without risk of distortion. Technical experts must be listened to with respect. Nevertheless, no ethical issue is purely technical. Ethical questions force us to choose among comparable alternatives. The proper function of the technical expert is to clarify those alternatives. But, as a technical expert, he cannot resolve the deeper ethical question as to which of the alternatives is *morally* best. To illustrate this point from the field of medical ethics, in recent years there has been considerable discussion of therapeutic abortions. Medical science has a great deal of valuable information on the technical side. It can tell us when an abortion may be necessary to save the life of the mother or when it may be desirable for the sake of her physical or mental health. It can help us decide whether or not the fetus may be deformed in some hopeless way. It can outline for us the different methods of abortion and it can predict the physical consequences of abortion at different stages of a pregnancy. All this is useful information. But when we try to decide whether or not to legalize abortion and whether or not to advise abortion in a particular case, we are confronted with a moral decision. Even physicians, who are the medical experts, have to go beyond their expertise in their own decisions concerning abortion, euthanasia, and the transplantation of vital organs. After the technical side of issues has been clarified we have to make final decisions on the basis of ultimate values. We should be leery of attempts to bypass technical problems. But we must also be watchful of efforts to use the aura of expertise or the language of the technical to cloud moral decisions or to undermine our self-confidence in approaching them.

Such things must be said in a book of this kind, which deals with a problem in economic ethics. The central, overriding concern of this small volume is to make it easier for people (who may or may not be economists or ethical theorists by profession) to participate in the new American discussion of the guaranteed income proposals. The central issues, as we have said, are ethical. They have wide ramifications. Here, if anywhere in modern life, persons of moral sensitivity can address an important public question with relevance and effect. Moreover, the way in which America deals with this moral problem will affect other issues and the moral climate in general.

Despite this, it is perhaps curious that we should be occupied with the question of guaranteed income at all. Our society has become the wealthiest in the history of mankind. Prosperity rises from strength to strength. Annual increases in the gross national product exceed $40 billion. Technological change releases more and more people from direct physical labor in the productive process, to such a point that some experts now claim that less than 10% of the population may eventually be able to produce the material goods needed by the rest. Yet, despite such wealth and productivity, 30 million people can be defined as impoverished, and many people can consider it to be immoral to do anything directly to change their condition. Suppose we all lived in some Garden of Eden, with all the conditions of life as plentiful as the air we breathe. Would we find something intrinsically immoral in this? Would we feel that such beneficence should be rationed out on the basis of deserving? Why, then, should there be a question about making provision for all the people in the distribution of the increasing prosperity of our land?

Of course the issues are not quite so simple. Even though the debate over the poverty problem and the guaranteed income idea fairly bristles with paradox and irony, there are hard ethical questions which need to be faced honestly. If our moral conception of work, the so-called "Protestant ethic," has reached out of the past with a heavy hand to control our decisions, it cannot be dismissed lightly. Inherited values must be understood, and their moral relevance must be conserved. Nevertheless, we must free ourselves and our culture from those aspects of inherited values and practices which stand in need of correction.

Ethical viewpoints rest upon more ultimate commitments. Most of the views expressed in this book are broadly based upon interpretations of the Hebrew-Christian tradition. This tradition has had such an enormous influence in the shaping of our civilization that even avowed atheists and "post-Christians" tend to assume its humanistic values. This fact undoubtedly facilitates conversation and consensus across religious lines. At the same time, however, we need to be as clear as we can about the sources of our moral judgment. At certain points (such as in the use of the doctrine of grace in Chapter III) the discussion will be based more explicitly on the Christian faith. But this does not mean that only Christians have significant things to say regarding issues of economic ethics. The guaranteed income proposals need to be discussed and decided by all of us, and it would be gratifying to learn that non-Christians as well as Christians have been helped in some way by this book.

Chapter I

A RADICAL NEW POSSIBILITY

"From the inevitable laws of human nature some human beings will be exposed to want. These are the unhappy persons who in the great lottery of life have drawn a blank."

With these cheerful words, Robert Malthus provided his own personal agreement with the notion that the poor we will always have with us. Certainly this has been the majority report of human history. Morally sensitive people, including Malthus, have always deplored poverty. But they have not been able to erase the hard facts of economic scarcity. Expression of moral concern has never been enough, as Victor Hugo illustrates. In the preface to *Les Misérables* he wrote that "so long as ignorance and wretchedness exist on the earth, books like this cannot be useless." It was a good and useful book; but even books like that still could not overcome the fundamental problem: if there is not enough to go around, some will go without. The perennial fact of material scarcity is why economics has been called the dismal science.

But the economic facts are no longer so gloomy. Hard figures indicate a changed situation, at least so far as our society is concerned. The present gross national product (the figure representing the aggregate of goods and services produced in one year) is now over $800 billion, which represents an average of about $4,000 for every one of the 200 million men, women, and children in America. This gross national product (GNP) is growing at the rate of about $40 billion per year. The GNP will be more than a trillion dollars before 1975 according to conservative estimates. With such resources, poverty surely is no longer *necessary*.

This point can be illustrated with a thought experiment: It is estimated that about 30 million Americans still live in poverty, when poverty is defined as an annual income less than $3,000 for a family of four. Suppose each of these 30 million people (men, women, and children) were simply *given* $1,000 per year. A family of four would have an income of $4,000, a family of six would have $6,000, and so on—well above the poverty line. Total cost to the nation would be around $30 billion per year. This $30 billion would be less than the size of the annual increase in the gross national product. That is to say that if we were to decide to do this next year, we would at the end of next year still have a larger GNP left over than we had this year. Disregarding other variables, present levels of wealth would remain essentially untouched.

I have not suggested this thought experiment because I believe that the problem of overcoming poverty is as simple as this. There are good practical reasons for not using this particular amount and for allowing different-sized grants for heads of households and their dependents. Any particular plan of guaranteed income grants would have to be much more carefully refined in order to safeguard the interests of recipients, of society, and of the economy. But the point I do wish to underscore is that scarcity—the simple lack of wealth—is no longer one of those good practical reasons. We have more than enough wealth, and we are growing wealthier by the year. As a matter of simple arithmetic, one could seriously question President Johnson's judgment that the various guaranteed income plans "are almost surely beyond our means at this time." This assertion, which he made in the Economic Report to the Congress, in January, 1967, has to be seen as a reflection of the political difficulties of adopting a guaranteed income plan—not as a valid judgment of what the nation could or could not afford economically.[1]

In view of the changed situation, a variety of different guaranteed income proposals have been made by economists, wel-

[1] In context, the President's statement was doubtless a political feeler. He did express interest in the concept of guaranteed income and indicated his desire to appoint a study commission on the subject.

fare experts, and political leaders. All these proposals are based, more or less, on a radical new concept: namely, that we "fight poverty" at the root by guaranteeing some minimum basic income for all our citizens, regardless of the reasons for their poverty. Instead of worrying first about such things as incentives, psychological maladjustments, family disorganization, or the need for job retraining, it is proposed that government should deal with the need for money by giving it directly to those who need it. According to most of the proposals, a minimum basic income would be guaranteed as a legal right—an economic equivalent to the right of freedom of speech and religious liberty. In principle this is not so utterly alien to our tradition since we acknowledge the inalienable right of all our people to "life," as well as "liberty and the pursuit of happiness." Indeed, none of these rights can have substance without provision for the means of life itself. According to these proposals the needed basic income would be granted regardless of whether one was willing to work to earn it. It would represent a kind of economic floor below which nobody would have to fall.

Background of the New Proposals

Such a concept is a bit startling, both in its simplicity and in its radical novelty. But the idea of a guaranteed income for all is not entirely new, and most of the specific proposals which have been offered contain many links with presently accepted practices. Not surprisingly, the idea has appeared now and again in the writings of utopian social thinkers, such as Edward Bellamy. One variation of the idea, the so-called "Speenhamland system" was in operation for a number of years in England before it was finally abolished by the Poor Law of 1834. The Speenhamland approach provided a floor of economic security which was based upon family size and the price of wheat. It was guaranteed regardless of the work pattern of the laborers who benefited by it, and, not surprisingly, one of the reasons for its failure was the fact that employers began using it as an excuse for lowering wages.

The twentieth century has not seen any experiment quite like this, although we have witnessed the rapid development of the "welfare state." Most present-day countries are welfare states to

21

some degree, even when their ideologies stress individualism and free enterprise capitalism. It is very widely believed that government has the ultimate responsibility of guaranteeing certain minimum levels of physical and social well-being. Welfare state programs generally represent direct provision of health services, financial grants based upon social security-type insurance schemes, and welfare relief provided on a casework basis. Direct income grants, not based on social insurance programs or a case-oriented "means test," have yet to be experimented with. (A number of countries now provide family allowances—an approach which will be discussed below.)

Recently, however, the guaranteed income idea has begun to catch hold. During the 1940's Lady Juliette Evangeline Rhys-Williams proposed a universal "social dividend," which was to be a flat grant to all Englishmen regardless of their economic circumstances. Since taxation would recover most of the social dividend of the prosperous, this concept really represented a guaranteed minimum income for the poor. The idea of a negative income tax, according to which persons would be paid the amount of their unused income tax exemptions, was advanced by economist George Stigler in a 1946 article.[2] A scattering of other writers, notably including John Kenneth Galbraith,[3] make some reference to the idea during the 1950's. In 1962 Milton Friedman's book, *Capitalism and Freedom* strongly supported the negative income tax and developed it carefully. Robert Theobald's 1963 book, *Free Men and Free Markets* developed the guaranteed income concept from a very different perspective. A subsequent edition of this volume and numerous other writings have established him as one of the foremost exponents of the new idea.

[2] "The Economics of Minimum Wage Legislation," *American Economic Review*, XXXVI (June, 1946), 365. For a good summary of some of the historical background of guaranteed income proposals see Christopher Green, *Negative Taxes and the Poverty Problem* (Washington, D. C.: The Brookings Institution, 1967), esp. pp. 51-61, and Robert Theobald, ed., *The Guaranteed Income* (Garden City, N. Y.: Doubleday Anchor, 1967, 1966), esp. pp. 15-37.

[3] *The Affluent Society* (Boston: Houghton Mifflin, 1958). "An Affluent society, that is also both compassionate and rational, would, no doubt, secure to all who needed it the minimum income essential for decency and comfort." P. 255.

22

In 1964 the "Ad Hoc Committee on the Triple Revolution," a group of prominent liberal Americans, published a pamphlet which strongly supported the concept. Then, in 1966 a number of official and unofficial groups added their endorsement. Representative of these was a statement by the National Commission on Technology, Automation, and Economic Progress declaring that "we are convinced that rising productivity has brought this country to the point at last when all citizens may have a decent standard of living at a cost in resources the economy can easily bear." Although the Commission focused on the problem of helping people to earn their income through work, it went on to acknowledge that income maintenance would need to cover those for whom work was not much of a possibility: "The war on poverty has made it abundantly clear that the road to a satisfying life through work is not open to everyone: not to families without breadwinners, not to those whose productivity is reduced by physical or mental incapacity, not to people too old to work." [4]

Similar conclusions were expressed by the President's Council of Economic Advisers, the Office of Economic Opportunity, and the White House Conference on Civil Rights. Also in 1966, an impressive group of leaders of civil rights, labor, and religious groups published what it called the "Freedom Budget." The "Freedom Budget" proposed a massive national attack upon poverty in the United States. This was to be financed by budgeting a part of the probable increases in Gross National Product between 1965 and 1975. Total cost of this massive attack upon all phases of poverty was estimated at $355 billion over a ten-year period. The group suggested that this would be only about one-seventh of the total economic *growth* between 1965 and 1975. While the "Freedom Budget" group was more interested in the attainment of full employment and in a concerted attack upon problems in housing, education, and health, it also supported guaranteed income: "There is need for gradual elimination of the whole patchwork of *ad hoc* public assistance programs, which are highly inefficient and costly relative to their results and which tend toward

---

[4] *Technology and the American Economy: Report of the National Commission on Technology, Automation, and Economic Progress* (Washington, D. C.: 1966), p. 38.

pauperization of recipients, and development of a guaranteed income on a nationwide basis." [5]

Since 1966 interest in guaranteed income has been spreading. An informed discussion is proceeding in economic, labor, business, welfare, and religious circles.[6] At this time of writing, national attention has been diverted by the expensive conduct of war in Southeast Asia. But renewed public debate of the guaranteed income concept is likely to occur as national attention returns to urgent domestic priorities. Discussion then will need to focus upon the different types of proposals and upon the moral issues with which we will be occupied principally in this book.

We cannot here give a complete analysis of each of the proposals. Nevertheless, we must recognize that there *are* a variety of *different* concepts being discussed. A person who is exposed to only one of these may dismiss the whole idea just because of difficulties with that one proposal. But these difficulties may be surmounted in other approaches. For example, some proposals make careful provision for economic incentives to work, while others consider this undesirable. Moreover, some awareness of the main variations will help us in discussing the moral issues, since the

---

[5] A "Freedom Budget" for All Americans (New York: A. Philip Randolph Institute, 1966), p. 63.

[6] Christopher Green, Negative Taxes and the Poverty Problem, is the best technical introduction to this discussion. Robert Theobald, ed., The Guaranteed Income: Next Step in Socioeconomic Evolution? contains informed essays by scholars representing a wide variety of fields—thus providing an excellent introduction to noneconomic as well as economic implications of the idea. Still another good introduction is provided by Proceedings of the National Symposium on Guaranteed Income (Washington, D. C.: The Chamber of Commerce of the United States, 1966), which contains important summary viewpoints by Robert Theobald, Milton Friedman, James Tobin, Henry Hazlitt, and Thomas Curtis. Several periodicals have devoted whole issues to viewpoints on guaranteed income. Among these are American Child (Summer, 1966), Industrial Relations (February, 1967), and Social Action (November, 1967). The Ad Hoc Committee for Guaranteed Income at the University of Chicago's School of Social Service Administration publishes Guaranteed Annual Income Newsletter, which is entirely concerned with the issue. It is being discussed occasionally in a wide variety of periodicals, among which the following might be cited in particular: The Public Interest, Business Week, The Nation, The New Republic, Christianity and Crisis, Welfare in Review, Social Work, and The New York Times Magazine. Articles are also beginning to appear with increasing frequency in the mass circulation periodicals.

different approaches to some extent raise different kinds of moral questions.

Therefore, I shall use the remainder of this chapter to highlight some of the main proposals which are now being discussed.

Robert Theobald's "Basic Economic Security"

In order to appreciate Robert Theobald's proposals fully, it is first necessary to see their background in his view of what is happening in the American economy. In his various writings,[7] Theobald stresses the revolutionary meaning of cybernation (which means, generally speaking, the combination of automated machinery with computers). He believes this revolution will make our inherited ideas about work quite obsolete. Fewer and fewer people will be needed to handle production. Structural unemployment will grow and it will affect not only the laboring classes but also persons in white collar or executive positions whose intellectual labor can be replaced by computers. We therefore face a new kind of crisis. In the first place, the crisis involves the economic insecurity of large numbers of people whose whole way of life is threatened. This insecurity strikes the poor most immediately, but it is also beginning to strike the middle-class persons whose economic and social commitments can be undermined almost overnight by loss of income. Secondly, the crisis threatens the foundations of the free market. When large numbers of people do not have adequate purchasing power, overproduction and economic slump can recur. We may again, as in the great depression of the 1930's, face the paradox of widespread poverty in the presence of abundant resources and unused productive capacities. Thirdly, the crisis threatens democratic political institutions, for economically insecure people are not able to participate freely and responsibly in the political process. Finally, the crisis is a moral one. It raises the question whether we are prepared to guarantee the economic basis of human dignity for all.

[7] See esp. *Free Men and Free Markets* (Garden City, N. Y.: Doubleday Anchor, 1965, 1963) and *The Challenge of Abundance* (New York: Clarkson N. Potter, 1961). He has also summarized his views in various articles and papers.

Theobald believes that the era of cybernation is not just another phase of industrialization. He does not believe that it will, in the long run, open up many additional jobs as past advances in technology have done. Rather, he considers it to be a new stage in the evolution of man's economic development. It is something like man's advance from a farm and handicraft economy into the industrial revolution. This new stage, like the former, could be liberating for man. But if we insist upon tying income to work, as in the past, we will miss our opportunity. We will become slaves to our new productive capacities instead of making them our servant. Theobald believes we are entering an era in which cybernation will be able to do for our civilization what the slaves did in liberating the leisure class of ancient Greece to become truly creative. He does not believe that we need to worry about using economic incentives to encourage people to work. In the first place he believes that most Americans are so habituated to work that they would not leave the source of their sense of social worth just because of a guaranteed income base. In the second place, he argues that modern psychological theory has shown that people are actually more motivated to strive for self-fulfillment after their basic needs for food, clothing, and shelter are met. There is, he writes, "increasing rejection among psychologists of the thesis that man will not act unless compelled to do so by positive or negative sanctions." [8]

What, then, are his specific proposals?

First, he suggests a guaranteed minimum income for all, as a matter of constitutional right. This he calls "Basic Economic Security." (As a starting point, he suggests a minimum guarantee of $1,050 for each adult and $650 for each child, with an annual increase of 5% to take the rate of productivity and normal inflation into account.) *In Free Men and Free Markets,* Theobald proposed that people receiving Basic Economic Security might also be allowed to keep 10% of what they earn through jobs, but in his more recent writing he seems to reject this form of incentive.

Secondly, he calls for supplements to the income of those in the middle income group who are thrown out of work by tech-

[8] "Guaranteed Income: Short and Long-run Issues," in *Guaranteed Annual Income Newsletter* (May-June, 1967), p. 2.

nological advances. He calls this plan "Committed Spending," because it is a device to help such people keep their commitments to spend at particular levels. This would make it possible for a family with an income of, say, $9,000 per year to maintain its economic and social commitments at nearly the same level. "Committed Spending" would allow this family a "reasonable proportion of their average income over a reasonable period of time in the past."

Thirdly, he proposes the development of "Consentives," which he defines as "any nonprofit-oriented productive organization whose members consent to work together while receiving due-incomes under the Economic Security Plan." [9] According to this intriguing idea, persons would be able to band together to create things (art, craft-objects, dramas and music, etc.) which could be sold on the open market. If the venture were successful in economic terms, its members might be able to derive their income from this new source rather than from guaranteed income. Otherwise, money gained from this source would simply go to repay government for the guaranteed income. The "Consentive" would be an opportunity for creative activity in the context of a free market economy.

While so brief a summary can scarcely do justice to Theobald's views, it may at least introduce them. So far as the economics of personal income and work are concerned, Theobald's position is probably the most radical of those supporting guaranteed income. It should not simply be dismissed for that reason, but we may now look at several other proposals which are more continuous with present practices.

The Negative Income Tax

The Negative Income Tax conception is today most associated with the name of Milton Friedman. He disagrees sharply with Theobald's interpretation of the meaning of cybernation. Friedman argues that new forces of automation and cybernation do not represent a radically new era; instead, they are a continuation of

[9] *Free Men and Free Markets*, p. 165.

the industrial revolution. He asserts that unemployment resulting from new productive forces will always, in the long run, be more than compensated for by the opening up of new forms of employment. The basic problem, therefore, is that of preparing the work force for the more sophisticated demands which will be placed upon it. In the long run, education and job training are the answer because today's unemployment is only a temporary dislocation.

Why, then, does Friedman support a guaranteed income concept?

Because he does recognize the need for adequate provision for the incurably poor and because he believes that present welfare measures, doled out on a demeaning casework basis, undermine the moral integrity and self-respect of those who receive it. Friedman also stresses another point: that is his desire to abolish most existing welfare measures (including aid to dependent children, old-age assistance, social security benefit payments, farm price supports, public housing, and other subsidies—but excluding veterans' payments). He estimates that more than $30 billion is being poured into such programs, and he believes that by using guaranteed income as a substitute billions of dollars could be saved. To illustrate this last point, he has written that "a program which *supplemented* the incomes of the 20 percent of the consumer units with the lowest incomes so as to raise them to the lowest income of the rest would cost less than half of what we are now spending." [10]

The main features of Friedman's proposal are as follows:

1. A federal subsidy should be given to everybody whose income falls below the amount of their income tax exemption (and standard deductions). The basic minimum income would be based upon some percentage of the standard income tax exemption of $600, the amount to be determined by "what the community could afford." Friedman himself speaks most frequently of 50% of the standard exemptions and deductions. For a family of four, this would involve a basic minimum income of $1,500.

2. Recipients would be permitted to retain some percentage

[10] *Capitalism and Freedom,* p. 194.

(perhaps 50%) of the income they earn in addition to their basic grant—up to the "break-even" point where the proportion of their income they were not permitted to keep equaled the amount of the subsidy. The other 50% of their income would be "taxed," thus reducing the size of their unearned grant. Using Friedman's figures as an illustration, the break-even point would be reached when a breadwinner for a family of four earned $3,000. Anybody earning more than $3,000 would then begin to *pay* taxes. The following simple table may help to illustrate further how this would work:

Family's Gross Earned Income	Net Amount of Grant to Family	Family's Total Net Income
$ 0	$1,500	$1,500
500	1,250	1,750
1,000	1,000	2,000
2,000	500	2,500
3,000	0	3,000

Thus, it will be observed, the recipient of guaranteed income still has a strong economic incentive to earn additional income since it will add to his net income.

3. The program should be administered by the Internal Revenue Service, thus permitting us to dismantle the whole welfare-dispensing apparatus.

Friedman summarizes the advantages of his Negative Income Tax proposal in the following way:

It gives help in the form most useful to the individual, namely, cash. It is general and could be substituted for the host of special measures now in effect. It makes explicit the cost borne by society. It operates outside the market. Like any other measures to alleviate poverty, it reduces the incentives of those helped to help themselves, but it does not eliminate that incentive entirely, as a system of supplementing incomes up to some fixed minimum would. An extra dollar earned always means more money available for expenditure.[11]

[11] *Capitalism and Freedom*, p. 192.

As a conservative political economist, Friedman points out that his proposal "offers a platform from which an effective political attack can be launched on existing undesirable programs." [12]

A number of other eminent American economists have made alternative negative income tax proposals. (James Tobin, Robert J. Lampman, and Leon Keyserling could be mentioned in particular.) Some of these proposals suggest higher or lower percentages of income which recipients should be permitted to retain. Some are thinking in terms of more generous basic grants. Tobin and most of the other economists totally disagree with Friedman concerning the desirability of doing away with present programs. Some economists also stress an interesting question of justice in relation to the "negative" tax: they believe that a person should receive from government the amount of his unused exemptions and standard deductions as a matter of equity. (With Friedman it is more a matter of convenience.) They argue that present tax laws discriminate against those earning less than the exemption figures since only those who earn above those figures get any benefit from them.

However, most of those who believe in the Negative Income Tax wish to use the normal income tax machinery for implementation, and most of them also agree on the importance of allowing recipients to keep some portion of their earned income as an incentive to work. Most would concur with Walter Williams and James M. Lyday's summary of the case for Negative Income Tax:

It can be universal in coverage but inexpensive to administer. It can furnish realizable incentives for program recipients to escape from poverty. Further, the system can be structured to avoid the invasion of privacy so pervasive to the existing income-maintenance programs under public assistance. Finally, a device such as the negative income tax will increase government outlays in periods in which the economy is slowing down and automatically reduce such outlays as the economy recovers.[13]

---

[12] *Proceedings of the National Symposium on Guaranteed Income* (Washington, D. C.: Chamber of Commerce of the United States, 1966).

[13] "The Case for a Negative Income Tax," in *American Child* (Summer, 1966), p. 18.

The Social Dividend

The social dividend idea is not really different (mathematically) from the Negative Income Tax, but it is based upon a somewhat different rationale.[14] It involves a basic grant, or subsidy, which is to be given to everybody, rich and poor alike. Since everybody is to receive the grant, no question can be raised about government favoring the poor over the rich. However, the amount of the social dividend is included in taxable income. This means that the poor will be able to keep most of theirs while the well-to-do will immediately return most of theirs to government in the form of increased taxes. For most people it would tend to be only a paper transaction. The net effect of the program upon the non-poor would then depend entirely upon the existing tax rates and the extent to which these tax rates were graduated.

At first glance, the cost appears staggering. For example, if $3,000 were provided for each family of four, the gross cost would be in the neighborhood of $165 billion. Or if the figure were set at $50 per month per person, the gross cost would be around $120 billion. As one expert in the U. S. Department of Health, Education, and Welfare puts it, such a plan clearly seems to be "outside the boundaries of the relevant." [15] But most of the "gross cost" would be recovered in the increased income tax returns. In the final analysis, the social dividend plan amounts to the same thing (mathematically speaking) as the Negative Income Tax, provided the income tax structure were appropriately adjusted.

Family Allowances

A more limited plan calls for income grants to families on the basis of the number of children.[16] As normally proposed, family

[14] For an excellent discussion of the mathematical implications of both approaches, see Christopher Green, *Negative Taxes and the Poverty Problem*.

[15] Helen O. Nicol, "Guaranteed Income Maintenance: Another Look at the Debate," in *Welfare in Review* (June-July, 1967), p. 8.

[16] For further background on the family allowance approach, see James Vadakin, *Family Allowances* (Miami: University of Miami Press, 1959), Alvin L. Schorr, *Poor Kids: A Report on Children in Poverty* (New York: Basic Books, 1966), Eveline M. Burns, "The Case for Family Allowances," in *Social Action* (November, 1967), pp. 19 ff., and Daniel P. Moynihan,

allowances would go to all families with children regardless of affluence or poverty. It thus is similar to the social dividend plan, except that grants are made only to children. There is an interesting logic behind this. Wages and salaries are based upon the work of individuals. But income is utilized on the basis of consuming units—generally families. At present there is no way for society to equalize the economic situation of small and large consuming units whose breadwinners are doing substantially the same thing. A number of writings on the "just wage" (including some of the papal encyclicals) have argued that wages should be based upon the amount needed to maintain a family. According to this view, wages should not simply be the amount earned by individuals or the amount needed to maintain individuals. But this judgment cannot be implemented by employers in a society where wage costs must be determined by work output—unless some adjustment can be made which does not change the employer's competitive position in the marketplace. The idea of family allowances is partly an effort to make such an adjustment, with costs being borne by the whole society. As generally proposed, the payments would be made to every child, irrespective of family income. The grant might or might not be included in taxable income and it might or might not involve elimination of present tax exemptions. One way or another, costs of such a program would have to be borne by the more prosperous. Wealthier families would probably see their grants disappear through taxation, as in the social dividend plan.

One proposal would involve payment of $50 per child under six years of age, and $60 per child from six to eighteen. Daniel Moynihan has recently given strong support for family allowances, although the specific figures he proposes would be only around $8 per month for children under age six and $12 per month for those who are older. Moynihan's figures would add no more than $288 to the annual income of a family of four. Obviously any particular set of figures could be substituted for these.

It is worth mentioning that family allowances are now provided by more than 60 countries. The United States is the only

---

"The Case for a Family Allowance," in *The New York Times Magazine* (February 5, 1967).

industrialized nation in the Western world without such a program. France, in particular, has made this a major element in its economic policy. And evidence from France, Sweden, and other countries employing this scheme indicates that family allowances do not appreciably affect the birth rate.

Guaranteed Income Without Money

The concept of providing guaranteed income "in-kind" can be included here, not because it is being discussed very much but because it demonstrates a significant point of view. Of course some relief programs (such as those involving surplus food and second-hand clothing) are of this sort. But these programs are not universal in scope, and they are administered in such a way that the recipient's inferior status is emphasized. What I have in mind, rather, is an intriguing proposal by Erich Fromm. Fromm suggests that in the present age of abundance society ought simply to make the actual necessities of life (food, shelter, clothing) available without charge.[17] As an illustration, he wonders whether we couldn't have the state pay the bakeries for all the bread they produce and let people help themselves to this necessary food item. Would the greedy take more than they could use? Fromm agrees that they might at first. But he believes that in the condition of abundance consumption would soon correspond to need (as in soda fountains, where, after a couple of weeks of gorging themselves on ice cream, employees reputedly restrain themselves). Fromm, like Robert Theobald, is impressed by the potential abundance of all real necessities of life. But, as a psychologist, he is also concerned about the increasing tendency for people to make economic consumption the be-all and end-all of human existence. He distinguishes between the objectives of "maximal consumption" (consuming all you can) and "optimal consumption" (consuming what you *need* to consume), and he believes that social policy should aim toward the latter rather than the former.

At the same time, he proposes "a vast change in industry from

[17] See Erich Fromm's essay on "The Psychological Aspects of the Guaranteed Income," in Robert Theobald, ed., *The Guaranteed Income.*

the production of commodities of individual consumption to the production of commodities for public use." The latter includes such things as facilities for education, the cultivation of art, drama and music, public health and medicine, and transportation, parks, and libraries. All these he considers more fundamental to the realization of man's true nature than luxury gadgets for private consumption.

Guaranteed Opportunity to Earn an Income

There are some who are sympathetic to guaranteed income proposals as a necessary means of eliminating poverty but who would prefer to base this upon work opportunities. This can be treated as a guaranteed income proposal only insofar as it represents a public commitment to provide everybody with an opportunity to earn an adequate income doing what he is capable of doing. Every "guaranteed opportunity" program needs to be scrutinized with care. Sometimes such program proposals do not really mean "*guaranteed* opportunity." Congressman Thomas B. Curtis has, for example, outlined what he calls "guaranteed opportunity to earn an annual income." [18] But his proposal is limited to various work training schemes, and it is based on the assumption that private enterprise will (with some government subsidy) be able to generate enough job opportunities. It is not really a proposal that there be universal opportunity for work, with government as "employer of last resort." It is mostly what we already have, only more of it.

The concept of the old CCC and WPA programs is a bit different. This concept is that if a person desires a job, society will commit itself to provide that job in one way or another. Bertrand de Jouvenel has pointed out that the Old Testament ideal was essentially of this sort. In ancient Israel the *basis* of income (the land) was made available to all. But if one wished to *have* any income he had to work the land in order to gain it.[19] President

[18] See "The Guaranteed Opportunity to Earn an Annual Income," in *Proceedings of the National Symposium on Guaranteed Income*, p. 60.
[19] *The Ethics of Redistribution* (Cambridge: Cambridge University Press, 1952), pp. 4-5.

Johnson gave his support to the concept of government as employer of last resort in late 1967, and the idea has strong support in the labor movement and elsewhere. Leon Keyserling favors such a governmental full-employment commitment, although he also favors the negative income tax at generous levels. Professor Frank Riessman, whose proposals will be discussed more fully in Chapter VI, goes further than most advocates of the guaranteed opportunity approach by suggesting large-scale governmental development of what he calls "new careers." Essentially this means job opportunities with possibilities of advancement and personal development.

Two Other Proposals

In the ongoing discussion of guaranteed income, two other proposals need to be understood in order to avoid needless confusion. The first is "categorical assistance," and the second is the "guaranteed annual *wage.*"

"Categorical assistance," as supported by Helen O. Nicol and other public welfare leaders, involves provision of income payments to people on the basis of their particular needs and problems. Where guaranteed income specifies minimum income grants to people below designated levels (regardless of age or physical, mental, or social condition), categorical assistance attempts to match payments to needs in a more refined way. As generally proposed, categorical assistance still requires considerable individual casework to determine the actual financial needs of clients. Of course, American society already has a great deal of categorical assistance built into its welfare concepts. But, in the context of guaranteed income discussion, those who favor this approach usually wish to broaden its coverage and refine its categories still further in an effort to deal with those poverty problems which cause others to favor the more radical guaranteed income proposals.

"Guaranteed annual wages" is a term which is often erroneously used interchangeably with "guaranteed income." The difference is that "guaranteed annual wages" refers to an annual rather than hourly or daily basis of wage payments in industry, while guaranteed income is provision of income whether or not one is working at all. The guaranteed annual wage idea has been discussed widely in the labor movement, particularly since World War II. Recently it was very largely adopted as part of the 1967 settlement between the United Auto Workers and the major automobile manufacturers. In effect, it involves payment of workers on the basis of salary rather than hourly wages, although in the UAW contracts it is possible for workers to earn more than the guaranteed minimum annual income, depending on the actual number of hours worked.

The Question of Practical Difficulties

It may occur to anyone who is exposed only to a brief summary of the more radical guaranteed income proposals that these ideas contain numerous practical difficulties. Most of their proponents would be the first to agree. Indeed, most of these proposals are being discussed and debated at exactly the point of their practicality. However, even for the uninitiated I believe that enough has already been said here to indicate that there are ways of dealing with guaranteed income so as to eliminate most of the difficulties which appear at first glance. For example, if one considers the incentive question to be a serious practical issue, we have already seen that the negative income tax scheme has made a solid practical effort to meet this kind of objection. Moreover, enough has been said to illustrate that our society should have no difficulty financing guaranteed income, although some plans would obviously be more costly than others. This kind of practical problem certainly is not important enough to foreclose adoption of *some* form of guaranteed income.

Furthermore, any fair judgment of practical difficulties has to take a searching look at the practical difficulties in all present programs designed to eliminate poverty. Or, to push this back still further, we cannot forget the impracticalities of poverty itself! It is impractical for the poor, and it is also impractical for the whole society. I suppose there is no public policy which is perfectly practical, but I also doubt that any of the proposals discussed in this chapter are totally impractical.

Nevertheless, morally sensitive people need to examine the concept of guaranteed income at a deeper level. Laying questions of practicality to the side for a moment, they need to ask the moral question: what are the basic ethical issues raised by the proposal of such economic guarantees? In particular, they must examine the moral implications of income without work—the proposal that some level of income should be provided as an absolute social right. Many of the so-called "practical questions" may finally be resolved, not on the basis of pragmatic considerations, but on the basis of root moral convictions.

In the next chapter, I shall open this discussion of the ethical question by outlining some of the most basic moral *objections* to income without work.

Chapter II

MORAL OBJECTIONS TO INCOME
WITHOUT WORK

In August, 1967, a Louis Harris survey showed that 60 percent of a cross section of Americans were opposed to a guaranteed income proposal. Only 28 percent positively favored the idea, with 12 percent who were not sure.

This instinctive response to an unexamined idea is revealing. The pollsters noted four main reasons given by the 60 percent (without, however, indicating how many listed each of these reasons). They were: "Pay too much welfare now." "Would encourage free-loaders." "Some would stop work altogether." "They can work if they want to." These reasons represent a mixture of moral and practical objections. But the point to which I wish to draw attention is the immediacy and the quality of self-evident assurance with which such objections are expressed. The idea of the value of work, the more or less competitive view of human society, the rewarding of effort alone—all present themselves to us as self-evident, and therefore unexamined, truth.

It may be that some of the practical objections to guaranteed income proposals are based upon this or that personal experience with "welfare" or "free-loaders." Or they may be based simply upon objection to paying taxes. But there is also this underlying sense of the *immorality* of giving people what they haven't earned. Such a moral sentiment is not easy to get at. This is partly because the feelings are on the axiomatic level where people are not used to thinking fresh thoughts. It is also because such attitudes are mixed with moral values of benevolence and generosity. We should avoid sweeping generalizations about our culture and its values. Nevertheless, we must attempt to get at the root of moral objections to guaranteed income, and this will require a brief interpretation of those objections as they appear in our inherited culture.

Economic Individualism

The individualistic theme is prominent in American attitudes toward work and income. A man must stand on his own two feet. Even the victims of vast, impersonal economic forces are likely to reflect the individualistic spirit. During the Great Depression, when millions were unemployed through no fault of their own, studies of individual workers revealed noticeable feelings of guilt and personal inadequacy. Many of the workers attributed their inability to find and hold jobs to their own lack of ability or character. Doubtless this sentiment was shared by industrialists, who also tended to view the matter in individualistic and moralistic terms. Even President Roosevelt, who was viewed by some as an enemy of free enterprise, insisted upon a largely individualistic definition of the problem of income. In the dark days of depression prior to becoming President, he asserted that "the dole method of relief for unemployment is not only repugnant to all sound principles of social economics, but is contrary to every principle of American citizenship and of sound government." American labor, he asserted, "seeks no charity, but only a chance to work for its living." [1]

The theme of individualism is often expressed in the writings of economists, particularly when they write on moral questions. For example, George J. Stigler plunges to the root of individualism in the following observations:

The supreme goal of the Western World is the development of the individual; the creation for the individual of a maximum area of

---

[1] *The Public Papers and Addresses of Franklin D. Roosevelt,* I (New York: Random House, 1938), 456. The address was delivered to the New York State Legislature in 1931.

personal freedom, and with this a corresponding area of personal responsibility. Our very concept of the humane society is one in which individual man is permitted and incited to make the utmost of himself. The self-reliant, responsible, creative citizen—the "cult of individualism" for every man, if you will—is the very foundation of democracy, of freedom of speech, of every institution that recognizes the dignity of man. I view this goal as an ultimate ethical value.[2]

Similarly, Professor Friedman comments that "we take freedom of the individual, or perhaps the family, as our ultimate goal in judging social arrangements." While Friedman believes that freedom has to be exercised responsibly in a social context, he goes on to assert that "the 'really' important ethical problems are those that face an individual in a free society—what he should do with his freedom." [3] He is *not* speaking here of what society might need to do, ethically, as a *whole*. The foundation norm is defined in terms of the individual.

The philosophy of individualism is well expressed in an advertisement which the Warner and Swasey Company placed in *Newsweek* on May 2, 1966. The advertisement (having nothing to do with the company's products) addressed itself to the declining importance of individual self-reliance in American society. It was in the form of a man's reflections about his childhood and how times have changed.

We never heard these modern phrases like "standard of living," "subsistence level," "minimum requirements." Our standard of living was whatever my father . . . earned. I don't suppose people "understood" me and if I had said so, my mother would have asked, "Why should they?" And certainly no one ever gave a thought to my "problems." They were mine, weren't they? Mine to solve. Why should I expect anyone else to bother?

If my father was laid off, we stopped spending on anything but food, and a lot less of that. My dad spent every waking hour looking for work—*any* work. We lived on savings and when they were gone, we moved in with relatives. If there had been no relatives, when every

[2] George J. Stigler, "The Proper Goals of Economic Policy," in *Journal of Business* (July, 1958), p. 714.

[3] Milton Friedman, *Capitalism and Freedom*, p. 12.

penny and every salable asset was gone, we would have gone to the only place left—the County Poor House—but that would have been an admission that we couldn't take care of ourselves.

. . . I guess we didn't have much. But we had something that was infinitely more important, infinitely more rewarding—we had self-respect, because whatever we had, however little it was, *we earned.*

Novelist-philosopher Ayn Rand expresses this attitude in her various writings ("I swear by my life and my love of it that I will never live for the sake of another man, nor ask another man to live for mine"), and it is also to be found in the writings of such figures as William Buckley and Barry Goldwater.[4] While some of the writings of this sort can be considered extreme, the individualistic attitude is actually an important part of the cultural climate in which we live. It probably affects all of us to some degree.

The "Protestant Ethic"

The whole complex of ideas and attitudes about work and economic individualism is commonly called the "Protestant ethic." The phrase was used by German sociologist Max Weber in *The Protestant Ethic and the Spirit of Capitalism,* which was a classical analysis of the relationship between Protestantism and the development of capitalism in Europe and America. The book has aroused much discussion in the half-century since its writing, and it will not be possible for us to enter into that discussion here.[5] For our purposes, Weber's study emphasized two early Protestant attitudes which helped shape the economic attitudes of the West in a decisive way. The first attitude is the positive view of work and the condemnation of idleness. It is largely rooted in the Prot-

---

[4] See, for example, Barry Goldwater, *The Conscience of a Conservative* (Shepherdsville, Ky.: Victor Publishing Co., 1960).

[5] It should be remembered, however, that Weber did not simply attribute capitalism to Protestantism (as if Protestantism had "caused" capitalism). Moreover, in his judgment the "spirit of capitalism" has long since "escaped from the cage" of its original relationship to Protestant Christianity. By the twentieth century it had become an essentially secular phenomenon. Max Weber would be the first to agree that many aspects of present-day economic individualism are far removed from the original spirit of Protestant Christianity.

estant doctrines of vocation, which view work as man's fitting response to God's grace. The second attitude is the somewhat ascetic attitude toward sensual pleasures and the enjoyment of wealth. While men ought to work hard, their work is for the glory of God and the public good—it is not simply for the sake of piling up riches for personal enjoyment. Weber believed that the curious combination of those two themes helps to explain why Western capitalism (at least in the earlier, formative period) emphasized both hard work and frugality. He takes Benjamin Franklin as a striking illustration. Franklin's little moral maxims on the importance of diligence, thrift, and prudence show a vastly different kind of capitalist spirit than one might expect in an out-and-out materialistic civilization. To waste a shilling becomes a moral offense, and to pass an hour in idleness is gross dissipation. By Franklin's time, these ideas were already largely secularized. But their moralistic overtones owe much to the earlier influence of Protestant Christianity.

Weber's points can be illustrated readily from the writings of both major and minor Protestant leaders. Luther, who believed that man should serve God in his appointed worldly tasks, wrote, "What you do in your house is worth as much as if you did it up in heaven for our Lord God. For what we do in our calling here on earth in accordance with His word and command He counts as if it were done in heaven for Him." (From the "Letter to the German Nobility.") John Calvin conceived of the "calling" in more radical terms as man's active effort to transform the world for the glory of God. While Calvin viewed man's salvation entirely as a matter of his being chosen by God to receive divine grace, work was a very important evidence of salvation—and the Calvinists were known by the diligence with which they worked for the glory of God. Calvinists may, unconsciously, have sought to prove to themselves that they were indeed among the elect whom God had chosen for salvation. Whether or not this uncharitable judgment is true, there is no question concerning the seriousness of their attitude toward work nor of their scorn for idleness and dissipation.

John Wesley, who was heavily influenced by Calvinism, inveighed unceasingly against idleness among the early Methodists: "So far am I from either causing or encouraging idleness,

42

but an idle person, known to be such, is not suffered to remain in any of our societies; we drive him out, as we would a thief or a murderer." [6] To this day, Methodist ministers are admonished by their *Discipline* to follow this Wesleyan attitude: "Be diligent. Never be unemployed. Never be triflingly employed. Never trifle away time; neither spend any more time at any one place than is strictly necessary."

Multiplied a thousandfold, these viewpoints express that aspect of the "Protestant ethic" which has now become embedded in the economic attitudes of our civilization. They help to account for the strong emphasis upon work and for the attitude that there is something wrong with economic gain at the expense of another man's toil. They help us to understand the lingering feeling that prosperous people generally have more character and moral fibre than the poor. It is but a short step from this to the view that the poor may, after all, deserve their poverty. Such ideas may be in conflict with other inherited cultural attitudes which stress charitable giving for the relief of distress. But whether or not there is any inconsistency here, our inherited attitudes typically demand that the recipients of charitable gifts humbly acknowledge their undeserved benefaction.

The Moral Case Against Guaranteed Income

The climate of such ideas is obviously inhospitable to the concept of guaranteed income. But we must now turn to some objections to the concept which are more specific. I shall suggest five such objections.

1. *The injustice of income without work.* A strong case can be made *against* guaranteed income on the basis of distributive justice. Those who favor the concept may believe that it represents greater justice for the poor, but opponents can argue that it would undermine justice instead. The apostle Paul appealed to a conception of justice in his famous advice to the Thessalonian Christians: "If any one will not work, let him not eat." Another biblical expression speaks to the same point: "Whatever a man

* Quoted by Walter G. Muelder, *Religion and Economic Responsibility* (New York: Scribner's, 1953), p. 43.

sows, that will he also reap." To take from some who have worked in order to give to others who have not raises immediate questions of deserving. Is this rendering to each man his just due? Some of the classical economists, who held a labor theory of value, were particularly impressed by this problem. Since they believed that economic goods were a result of specific inputs of labor, it could readily be considered "immoral" to take the fruits of the labor of some in order to provide income for those who have not contributed those inputs of labor.

What, then, about justice for those who have had no opportunity to work? This certainly puts the question of distributive justice in a deeper perspective, since many of the poor really have not had an adequate opportunity to earn their living. But it does not destroy the basic objection. The basic objection concerns the injustice of distributing income without work. Those who object to guaranteed income on this basis may well argue that our energies should be focused upon guaranteeing opportunity to earn an income, and that income should be strictly correlated with the value of work performed.

2. *The erosion of human creativity.* If guaranteed income does not exactly imply idleness, its proponents seem willing enough to finance it. What would this do to man's creative potentialities? Quite apart from any peculiarly Calvinist understanding of work, we must insist that real *human* life is never merely passive. To be an integrated self is to be active and creative. The purely passive person merely receives impressions and chance stimulations. He is symbolized by the passive spectator at the theater or athletic contest. He may become excited, and he may identify himself with the home team or the principal actors. But in the final analysis he is only watching. The real participants are other people, out there before his eyes. After a time even the watching becomes dull. We cannot forget that it is through goal-directed activity (work) that we focus our life energies in integrated personhood.

Some of the more extreme advocates of guaranteed income insist that we are now entering an era in which man will be able simply to "enjoy" life (the "new leisure") without concerning himself further over work. But the implied route to "enjoyment" is often a passive one; it is not active and creative.

Thomas Carlyle, who was about as sturdy a representative of

the "Protestant ethic" as one might wish to see, asserted that one could find serenity only through work and attention to duty—not through the vain quest for "happiness." He summarized his views in this striking passage (from *Sartor Resartus*):

Foolish soul! What Act of Legislature was there that *thou* shouldst be happy? A little while ago thou hadst no right to *be* at all. . . . Be no longer a Chaos, but a World, or even Worldkin. Produce! Produce! Were it but the pitifullest infinitesimal fraction of a Product, produce it, in God's name! 'Tis the utmost thou hast in thee: out with it, then. Up, up! Whatsoever thy hand findeth to do, do it with thy whole might. Work while it is called Today: for the Night cometh, wherein no man can work.

While Carlyle here reveals himself partly as a child of nineteenth-century "Protestant ethic" culture of the most exacting sort,[7] a strong case can be made for the universal validity of this statement. It belongs to the essence of man's humanity to be a creative, active, productive being.

In fairness, most advocates of guaranteed income (including Robert Theobald) do not have a passive understanding of man's nature. But such a social policy certainly would not *require* anybody to work. Even the plans (such as Milton Friedman's) which incorporate incentive features, do not require work as a basis for receiving the minimum income grants. Theobald as a matter of fact speaks rather glowingly of the desirable future spread of unemployment. What would this do to the creative potentialities of people? Will we simply create and finance generations of television viewers?

3. *The undermining of social fulfillment.* Even if one were to reject much of the foregoing as too individualistic (and neglecting man's social nature), a case can be made for the active nature of relationships. Relationship, in Christian perspective, is

[7] Carlyle was also reacting *against* the British utilitarians, who tried to reestablish the pleasure principle of hedonism as the basis of ethical theory (though in much refined form). He reminds us that a passive view of human nature is closely related to a hedonistic ethic. We can recall that one of the classical arguments against hedonism is the observation that the most genuine pleasures are not the ones we seek but rather are the pleasures which come as a by-product of our other activities.

the underlying reality of life. We belong to one another in God. Yet our relationships, which express our social nature, cannot find fulfillment simply in being. Simple *being*, apart from *expression* toward God and toward one's fellows, is nonsocial. We must experience together, but we cannot experience together without communication, expression, creation. This is the inner social meaning of work. Passivity is an individualistic phenomenon.

The point can be illustrated with respect to art. Regardless of comments such as "art for art's sake," art is a form of communication. A great artist (such as Rembrandt or Beethoven) will insist that his creativity is a very personal thing. And he will not lower his conception to the immediate taste of the multitude. Nevertheless, he hopes some will understand and respond to his vision. Most of us are not great artists, of course; but we also find it necessary to be creative in order to express our social nature.

But what happens when men are told that they need work no longer? Have the supporters of guaranteed income assumed too readily that people will find creative, fulfilling things to do? There is not enough factual evidence to answer this question for us. Such evidence as there is, drawn from early retirement programs, forced unemployment, public welfare, and the like, seems to indicate that people vary in their response to periods of time without employment. Some respond creatively and use their time to contribute to the betterment of their fellows. Others seek pleasure wherever they can find it. Still others simply do nothing. Is it not likely that the prime beneficiaries of guaranteed income would have a greater tendency to fall in the last two categories?

There is also another question concerning social fulfillment. Will guaranteed income create a permanent class division in our society? Gunnar Myrdal and others have warned us against the possibility of a new "underclass" developing in America. Myrdal writes that

for the larger part of America there is social and economic mobility through the educational system. Beneath that level a line is drawn to an "underclass." That class line becomes demarcated almost as a caste line, since the children in this class tend to become as poorly endowed as their parents.[8]

[8] *Challenge to Affluence* (New York: Random House, 1963), p. 38.

The problem is particularly acute, in his judgment, since many of those who make up this "underclass" have nothing to offer the economy: "As less and less work is required of the type the people in the urban and rural slums can offer, they will be increasingly isolated and exposed to unemployment, to underemployment, and to plain exploitation." [9] Myrdal is not an opponent of guaranteed income. Indeed this idea of an underclass can be used to support an economic minimum below which people should not be permitted to sink. But would guaranteed income divide society between the productive and the nonproductive, with socially destructive results? Could such a division become permanent? Could guaranteed income recipients inherit attitudes and pass them on to their own children, something like the so-called "third generation welfare recipient" problem?

Undoubtedly most people will be employed for the foreseeable future. What will their attitude be toward those who are simply drawing an income? And what will be the attitude of people who receive from society but who cannot point to any contribution they are making to society in return? To illustrate: John and Mary Smith are unemployed and draw guaranteed income. Their next-door neighbor Tom Jones is employed as an electrician, and his wife Ruth teaches school. What will these economic facts do to their social relationships? How will their children respond to each other? Is genuine community possible under such circumstances? This is the question.

4. *The incompetence and immorality of the poor.* Even if guaranteed income could survive the foregoing criticism, there remains the question of how it would be spent. Have we any moral right to assume that the poor will use their freedom responsibly? How do we know the money would not be used for immoral purposes?

Henry Hazlitt is particularly upset about this possibility. "The recipients," he writes, "are to continue to get this guaranteed income not only if they resolutely refuse to seek or take a job, but if they throw the handout money away at the races, or spend it on prostitutes, or whiskey, cigarettes, marajuana, heroin, or what-not."

[9] *Ibid.*, p. 49.

Furthermore, he adds, "they are to be given 'sufficient to live in dignity,' and it is apparently to be no business of the taxpayers if the recipient chooses nonetheless to live without dignity, and to devote his guaranteed leisure to gambling, dissipation, drunkenness, debauchery, dope addiction, or a life of crime." [10] Those who assume that poverty is related to immorality and undisciplined living might be quite impressed by this argument.

Even people who disagree with this judgment of the immorality of the poor might still believe that society ought to help the impoverished with their budgeting. They believe that the social caseworker ought to have a few levers at his disposal to help insure that income will not be misused. Stories abound of poor people who have color television sets while their children go without milk. A social caseworker who can control the flow of income can bring such foolishness to a halt. For instance, the food stamp plans now used in many states show how budgeting can be encouraged with a little pressure. Welfare recipients do not have to take their payments in food stamps, but every stamp will buy more food than the equivalent amount in cash. Use of the stamps increases purchasing power so long as food is being purchased.

Similarly, other localities have experimented with job-training requirements. In order to receive welfare funds, a recipient must agree to participate in a job-training or homemaking program. The welfare grant thus becomes a form of incentive for the development of greater social and economic competence. This concept is now required for participation in the Federal Aid to Dependent Children program.

Guaranteed income, established as a "right" would clearly decrease social control over the poor. It would thus make it more difficult for society to further the economic and moral education of these people.

5. *The need to overcome selfish inertia.* Among contemporary theologians, the interpretation of original sin as a universal tendency of men to put themselves first has found general acceptance. To be realistic about man, can we expect mere changes of economic relationships to change this aspect of human nature? But this is all the more reason why social structures, laws, and

[10] *Proceedings of the National Symposium on Guaranteed Income*, p. 56.

practices are needed to defend society against the disruptive effects of human sin. To be plain about it, it can be argued that man will avoid work even though he needs to be active and creative. Laziness can be counted upon as one of the common forms of self-centeredness. Economic rewards and punishments, social approval and social stigma may be needed to overcome the effects of man's all-too-prevalent tendency to avoid work and to exploit his fellows. Otherwise the production of the necessities of life may slacken and society may disintegrate without such external stimuli to overcome man's selfishness.

This kind of argument needs to be used cautiously, of course. If man is corrupted by selfishness, this fact is about as evident in the behavior of the wealthy as it is in the behavior of the poor. Nevertheless, the need to overcome inertia can be taken seriously as a moral argument against guaranteed income. The concept does seem to presuppose a rather idealistic view of human nature. Thinkers such as Theobald seem to believe that once basic economic security has been provided, the guaranteed income recipients will blossom forth with all kinds of altruism and creativity. It may be more likely, given a realistic view of human nature, that most people will simply milk society for all it's worth and let their fellows go hang. At best, will they not become lazy and shiftless?

On this kind of basis, a case can be made for economic incentives and social pressure as a morally "necessary evil" to overcome the selfishness in man's nature. Perhaps welfare recipients ought to be made to feel a twinge of shame—not because they are less important in the sight of God, but because this is necessary to break through their self-centeredness and inertia.

To summarize: a case can be made against guaranteed income on the ground of equity and justice, its damaging effects upon human creativity and social fulfillment, its overlooking the incompetence and immorality of the poor, and its neglect of the need to overcome man's selfishness and inertia. Most of these arguments are rooted in the assumptions of economic individualism and the "Protestant ethic" which are more or less taken for granted in our society. I have stated them here as persuasively as possible, even to the point of risking overstatement.

In the following chapter, I shall outline a Christian response to the assumptions upon which these arguments are based. In doing so, it will be necessary to agree with some of the points dealt with above; but they will need to be seen in a somewhat different perspective.

Chapter III

A CHRISTIAN RESPONSE TO THE "PROTESTANT ETHIC"

> When the Stranger says: "What is the
> meaning of this city?
> Do you huddle close together because
> you love each other?"
> What will you answer? "We all
> dwell together
> To make money from each other"? or
> "This is a community"?
>
> T. S. Eliot, *Choruses from "The Rock"*

The "Protestant ethic" continues to have great power among us—at least in its inherited form. It is the biggest stumbling block to our acceptance of any of the guaranteed income proposals because it raises doubts which are deeper than any of the practical problems. But having examined the moral case against guaranteed income in as convincing a manner as possible, we must now ask ourselves whether we really are convinced by it. Are we willing to settle for economic individualism? Is competition the real meaning of human community, or is there a deeper sense in which we are brothers and sisters in God's intended human family? Do we really believe that every economic benefit has to be "earned"? Are there not all kinds of economic and social benefits which none of us could possibly earn but which enrich our lives every day? Are we in any position to judge one another, in order to decide who

51

"deserves" and who does not deserve the right to basic economic existence? Is there not a bit of arrogance in this—a bit of playing God? Are we sure that the wealthy people are morally better than poor people? And if work is so necessary to man's personal and social fulfillment, why should we assume so unthinkingly that the poor will have to be manipulated in some way before they will be willing to put forth effort? Are the poor less interested in human fulfillment than other people?

To get at such questions requires deeper thinking than the more simplistic "folk logic" represented by many of the arguments in Chapter II. We shall discover, I think, that some of the points in this "folk logic" are valid. But we have to examine the moral issues posed by guaranteed income much more thoughtfully in order to put even these points in a balanced perspective.

In this chapter I shall attempt to outline a Christian response to that cluster of economic attitudes which is commonly called the "Protestant ethic." Since the remainder of the book will be based primarily on this chapter, it needs to be read with more care.

A Christian Understanding of Economic Good

We must begin with the real fundamentals. What, to the Christian, is the meaning of economic life?

There have been many conflicting interpretations of economic ethics among Christians. A periodical, which bears the self-confident title *Christian Economics,* identifies Christianity with economic individualism of the most unrestrained sort and suggests that *laissez faire* capitalism may be God's own economic system. At the other extreme, some Christian thinkers have identified socialism or communism as the best economic expression of Christian faith. Such economic views at both ideological extremes sometimes tend to subordinate the Christian faith, as such, to an economic system. But when we make an absolute out of *any* economic system we venture close to idolatry. It is an idolatry which is particularly appealing and particularly dangerous when the economic system happens to be one which best supports our own self-interest.

Therefore, the first thing a Christian ought to remember in evaluating alternative approaches to economic ethics is that his ultimate loyalty belongs to God, not to an economic system. And the second thing he must remember is to be suspicious of his own motives when his ethical views and his self-interest come together too closely.

When it comes down to the theological question, there are two extremes to be avoided. The first is the view that life is basically "spiritual" in the sense that economic questions do not matter. The second is the judgment that we can find real fulfillment as human beings through materialism.

The first view has been a constant temptation throughout Christian history. The early doctrinal struggles over Gnosticism involved this temptation. The Gnostics taught that reality is split between "good" and "evil" principles. They identified the good with reason and spirituality and the evil with material things. They considered the whole material world to be evil; indeed, they thought it the *source* of all evil. Some early Christians, such as Marcion, accepted this view. During the second century, Marcion and his many followers rejected the Old Testament and the God of the Old Testament because this God was pictured as Creator of the world. Marcionism, and similar heresies, were rejected because the mainstream of the church insisted that there is no difference between the God who created the physical world and the God revealed by Jesus Christ. The church thus asserted the goodness of this physical world, just as Old Testament teaching had done. But this has not been the end of the matter. Whenever Christians have used some vague spirituality as a way of avoiding economic questions, they appeal to a kind of Gnosticism. The most appropriate answer continues to be the goodness of creation and the Christian belief that the created world is more the reflection of God's purpose than the source of his frustration.

The other view, which embraces an out-and-out materialism, is also inconsistent with Christian faith. While the Christian regards material goods as good, he does not regard them as the source of meaning and value. It may help us to understand this if we follow the philosophical distinction between the "intrinsic" and the "instrumental." An intrinsic good is something which is good in and of itself. It is not something we use in order to get something

53

else. An instrumental good, on the other hand, is worthwhile because it helps us to achieve something else. It is an instrument or a tool, a means to some other end. Take the family automobile, for instance. While it may be "beautiful" in some sense (and while the advertisments may make us consider it an intrinsically good thing), the main thing about it is that it gets us where we want to go. A friendship, on the other hand, is not designed for something else. When we begin to "use" our friends as though they were merely tools to advance our selfish purposes, the intrinsic quality disappears and the friendship may be destroyed. Material objects are instrumental; they are the servants of other, intrinsic ends. When material objects are themselves considered to be intrinsic, materialism is the resulting life attitude. To understand the economic aspect of life, it is therefore necessary to comprehend the intrinsic ends which it is designed to serve. Only after we have identified these intrinsic ends are we in a position to judge economic arrangements. Those economic arrangements which best serve man's true (intrinsic) ends can be called good, while those economic arrangements which frustrate man's true ends must be considered inadequate or bad.

What are the intrinsic aspects of life?

We can speak of two which might be accepted by most thoughtful people, whether or not they are Christian. One is man's personhood. As an individual person, man is not to be viewed as some object or tool. His inner life is uniquely his own—no other man can duplicate or understand it exactly. Man is a self who experiences reality and who transcends his experience through knowledge and moral awareness. He is capable of choosing between good and evil, which is to say that to some extent he possesses internal freedom. The fulfillment of his potentialities as a unique person requires respect for his individuality and his freedom. We do not say that the individual human being exists merely to serve some other end. He is, as an individual self, not an instrumental means but an intrinsic end. This judgment, which was emphasized by the philosopher Immanuel Kant and by all subsequent personalists, is one of those moral axioms which cannot be proved. Either you accept it as axiomatic or you don't. But those who do not accept the inherent dignity and value of the individual human person thereby undermine the basis of their

54

own selfhood as well as that of others. It is of course important to remember that if persons are free they are capable of undermining the value of their own lives. They can treat themselves as things. They can turn their backs upon the responsible exercise of freedom, and they can disintegrate themselves through obedience to every chance whim or temptation. When we speak of individual personhood as an intrinsic end, we do well therefore to use the word *integrity* to describe it. The word integrity suggests the unity of the self (integration) and the fact that this unity is based upon man's own moral response. The word also suggests that, as an intrinsic good, personal integrity is not something which can be imposed upon another person. But every man possesses this possibility, and he must be treated accordingly.

But man is not isolated in his personal integrity. He is, as Aristotle said, a social being. The expression of his social nature, through mutual relationships with others, is also an intrinsic good. It is not just an instrumental means to something else; it is not even an instrumental means to man's personal integrity. The term mutuality conveys two truths which are easily overlooked. It reminds us of the necessary social dimension of human life—that life cannot be fully human in isolation. But it also suggests that this social dimension is not an impersonal one. Mutuality means common experience involving persons of integrity in relationship with one another. It incorporates respect for the integrity of others, and at the same time it acknowledges man's necessary involvement in the life of his fellows.

To put this in simpler language: there is something about man's individual personality which is intrinsically good, and there is something about his relationship with his fellows which is also intrinsically good. Man is both personal and social by nature.

Economic and political ideologies tend to neglect one or the other of these truths. Somebody will say that we ought to be rugged individualists. Somebody else will say that society is the only real thing and that persons are only parts of a whole, without any intrinsic meaning in and of themselves. But both these extreme understandings of the nature of man are false. When we make individualism the sole basis of human meaning, we destroy not only society but we also destroy the individual—for the solitary life-by-itself has no human meaning. (Of course, we do need to be solitary part of the time. But the *entirely* solitary or self-centered life is subhuman.) On the other hand, when we make society the sole basis of human meaning, we destroy not only the individual but we also destroy society—for society apart from individual persons in mutual interaction is not human society. You cannot destroy *either* the person or society without destroying the other at the same time.

To apply these judgments to our main question, then, true economic good can be seen as that arrangement of material goods which best supports and encourages integrity and mutuality. Economic questions need to be examined in this light *before* other questions of practicality are raised.

But a Christian theological perspective pushes us deeper than the terms "integrity" and "mutuality." This perspective requires us to ask, what is the *ultimate* meaning of life, and how does God's creation of the material world relate to it?

Karl Barth has provided a good theological formulation of the relationship between the intrinsic and instrumental which may help us grasp the basic problem of this book. Barth speaks of "creation as the external basis of the covenant" and "the covenant as the internal basis of creation." [1] God's covenant with man, through which God offers man a saving relationship with himself is what provides the meaning of life. But this covenant would not have been a possibility if God had not first created man and provided him with a world in which to exist. Both "covenant" and "creation" represent God's love, according to Barth. But the former could be described as the intrinsic good, and the latter could be termed instrumental. Creation represents all the conditions of existence which God has provided so that man's life can have concrete form. But creation is not, thereby, an intrinsic good. It exists only for the sake of man in his covenant with God. Creation is a necessary, but not sufficient, condition of their being an intrinsic good. The covenant, which is the intrinsic good, does not simply mean the mutual relationships among human beings who respect one another's dignity; it also means the divine-human

[1] *Church Dogmatics*, III/1, ed. G. W. Bromiley and T. F. Torrance (Edinburgh: T. & T. Clark, 1958). For an unusually perceptive interpretation of this formulation in a different setting, see Paul Ramsey, *Christian Ethics and the Sit-In* (New York: Association Press, 1961).

covenant which provides the ultimate meaning of human integrity and mutuality.

The word covenant is rich with biblical significance. The covenant between God and Israel is the basic theme of the Old Testament. It is this covenant which makes Israel into a community; because of the covenant Israel is no longer just an aggregate of individuals. As the covenant theme broadens out in later Hebrew and Christian interpretation, it is understood that God's covenant is with all mankind. The whole human family is God's intended covenant community. The word covenant suggests the quality of that community. A covenant is more than a contract between self-interested individuals, yet it is meaningless apart from the individuality of those who participate in it. Like the marriage covenant, it is entered into by responsible choice and with love, and through it one finds the fulfillment of one's whole being. The Christian faith affirms that it is God who has created us and who has summoned us to the life of fulfillment. In response to him, we acknowledge our involvement in the whole community of mankind. We do not identify our own well-being in opposition to that of others, nor can we even be merely indifferent to our fellows. To answer T. S. Eliot's question, we must define the meaning of the city as a loving community and not as a system of mutual exploitation.

Presently I shall attempt to develop this theme more fully. But notice what a difference it makes to see this covenant community under God as the basic, intrinsic reality which economic life is designed to serve. When we describe economic life as a necessary condition for this reality, we take economic questions very seriously. We understand them to reflect the more or less necessary conditions of God's whole plan for mankind. Deprivation of material goods can destroy life altogether. Lesser degrees of deprivation can undermine our ability to participate fully in the life of community. The root economic question for every Christian accordingly must be this: How can we structure the material conditions of life so that every man can find fulfillment in God's intended human community?

To be sure, the most ideal arrangement of material conditions imaginable is not in itself the Kingdom of God. It is possible, even likely, that the most ideal economic arrangements will continue to house a society of largely self-seeking persons. Economic arrangements per se are no *substitute* for genuine human community under God. Those who seek that community must continue to witness to its claim upon all of us. But a part of that witness must include action better to arrange the conditions of its possibility as an earthly reality. Jesus himself provides the model. According to the gospel traditions, he typically busied himself with such mundane chores as the healing of the sick and the feeding of the hungry. He did not consider the proclamation of the gospel as an adequate substitute for attention to the conditions of life. The Epistle of James puts the matter with fine irony: "If a brother or sister is ill-clad and in lack of daily food, and one of you says to them, 'Go in peace, be warmed and filled,' without giving them the things needed for the body, what does it profit?" (2:15-16.)

Before leaving the basic question of what we mean by economic good, I want to comment on our understanding of economic deprivation or poverty. Poverty needs to be understood in both an *absolute* and a *relative* sense. Absolute poverty may be defined as poverty which is serious enough to cause severe physical suffering and, in the extreme case, death. Relative poverty, on the other hand, is deprivation in the conditions of social existence serious enough to impede normal human relationships. When we speak of a "poverty problem" we do well to keep both forms in mind because both are morally significant. Physical suffering cannot be viewed as God's good intention, and it may even undermine personal integrity among the weak. Physical suffering is, in fact, nature's signal to us that the natural order of things has been upset in some way or that there are organic needs which need attention. Social deprivation, on the other hand, may create barriers between man and man which frustrate God's intended human community. Certain standards of consumption, including housing, clothing, transportation, and entertainment may actually be prerequisites to acceptance in social groups. (Incidentally, this social need may very well account for the tendency of some poor people to purchase expensive automobiles and clothing while neglecting nutritional and medical needs. There is a point at which acceptance by one's fellows in human community is more important to us even than physical health and survival.) Where some are affluent and others are deprived, the result may be equally dehumanizing attitudes of

58

inferiority among the deprived and arrogance among those who are not. Apparently this could be a moral problem even in the early church fellowship, as indicated by this little passage from the Epistle of James:

If a man with gold rings and in fine clothing comes into your assembly, and a poor man in shabby clothing also comes in, and you pay attention to the one who wears the fine clothing and say, "Have a seat here, please," while you say to the poor man, "Stand there," or, "Sit at my feet," have you not made distinctions among yourselves, and become judges with evil thoughts? (2:2-4.)

Both absolute and relative poverty help undermine God's intention for man, although poverty itself may refer only to economic conditions.

An adequate economic ethic therefore requires us to be aware of the whole range of economic issues, including the problems of production and the forms of distribution. We must be concerned about the overall adequacy of the supply of economic goods to serve human needs, and we must also be concerned about the effect of patterns of distribution of these goods as they affect human relationships in society.

Work and Leisure

The "Protestant ethic," as we have seen, views work as necessary and desirable. It sees work as an important part of Christian life. It views it as man's fitting response to God.

In discussing this theme in the preceding chapter, two points were stressed: first, that human life must be creative (not passive) if it is to be truly human; second, that work is necessary for social fulfillment and that a passive approach to life is basically individualistic. I believe that these are indeed valid statements, but they must be understood in a broader ethical perspective.

We must in the first place be clear about the meaning of work —and about the meaning of leisure. There are *broad* and *narrow* definitions of work, and there are *passive* and *active* definitions of leisure. It makes a great deal of difference which we mean when we discuss the ethical significance of "work" and "leisure." A *broad* definition of work sees it as any human activity directed toward the achievement of objectives. All creative exertion can be called work. On the other hand, a *narrow* definition of work views it only as a "job" which produces economic gain. In effect, a narrow definition of work is tied to the marketplace in our society. It is labor to produce goods and services which can be sold. To illustrate the difference, a housewife may devote many hours on the telephone to organizing a project for the P.T.A. This is an entirely voluntary activity for which she is paid nothing. Is it "work"? According to the broad definition it certainly is, for it is a human activity directed toward the achievement of an objective. But according to the narrow definition it is not, for she receives no economic reward.

There can also be two definitions of "leisure." A *passive* understanding of leisure equates it with idleness. Leisure is doing nothing, like somebody resting in the hammock or waiting in line. But leisure can also be viewed in an *active* sense. It can be seen as creative use of one's free time. Robert Lee suggests this distinction in his comments on the positive character of leisure:

Not everything one does in one's free time qualifies as leisure. Of course free time may be converted into leisure time. Hence *free time is only potentially leisure time.* Noncommitted or free time may well be idle time. The mood of leisure is affirmative, whereas the mood of idleness is negative. Idleness must not be confused with leisure, for idleness renders leisure impossible.[2]

In common usage, idleness is also called leisure; but the distinction is important.

These two understandings of work and leisure can be outlined in the following way:

1. *Work, broad definition:* any human activity directed toward achieving objectives, whether or not any remuneration is involved.

---

[2] *Religion and Leisure in America* (Nashville: Abingdon Press, 1964), p. 28. For other excellent discussions of the meaning of leisure, see Sebastian De Grazia, *Of Time, Work and Leisure* (New York: Twentieth Century Fund, 1962), and Charles Brightbill, *Man and Leisure: A Philosophy of Recreation* (Englewood Cliffs, N. J.: Prentice-Hall, Inc., 1961).

2. *Work, narrow definition*: activity for the sake of specific economic gains—a market definition of work.
3. *Leisure, passive definition*: idleness; "goofing off."
4. *Leisure, active definition*: active, possibly creative use of free time.

It will readily be seen from this outline that the first definition of work is broad enough to include the second definition of leisure. When leisure is defined actively and when work is defined broadly it can amount to the same thing. Robert Lee has in this regard pointed out that work and leisure in our society are becoming fused: "increasingly the distinction between the two has become tenuous." [3]

Simple attention to these distinctions can save much confusion in an ethical appraisal of work and leisure. If work per se is what is important in the Protestant ethic, then our definition of work cannot be limited to what is rewarded in the economic marketplace. It is the intrinsic character of the activity which has ethical significance. The question of economic rewards or distribution of income is *another* issue, which must be examined separately on its own merits.

Why is work, as such, morally important?

Various kinds of reasons have been given. It has been viewed as punishment (as the Genesis account seems to suggest). It has been considered a necessary form of discipline (as certain other biblical passages and the writings of various kinds of monastic orders assert). It can be viewed as a necessary evil (as the retirement advertisements imply). It can be seen as service to humanity; and it can be considered an act of response to God.

The first and the third of these were stressed in a little book on *Christian Faith and My Job*, written by Professor Alexander Miller a generation ago.[4] Miller argued that the primary rationale of work is its sheer economic necessity. "Work is to be done, first because it is necessary, and second in order that we may rest. It is not an end in itself." He emphasized the insight of Genesis that "work is part of the curse under which lies the whole of man's

---

[3] *Religion and Leisure in America*, p. 29.
[4] Alexander Miller, *Christian Faith and My Job* (New York: Association Press, 1946).

natural and social life." And he asserted that the various necessities of work "are all the real and inescapable conditions of man's life in the world, and there is no good in shutting our eyes to them." Therefore, the first real test of any form of work was, to Miller, whether it is necessary. Questions of creativity, or artistry, or craftsmanship are entirely secondary. Necessary work is to be done first, even if it is routine drudgery (as "much of the necessary work of the world is"). Our true calling, or vocation, is to match our capacity against the known needs.

If he were still living today, it would be interesting to hear Professor Miller's reassessment of work in the light of cybernation. He doubtless would continue to insist that even such new productive forces require hard and faithful and sometimes very routine labor if they are to meet man's actual needs. Possibly, however, he would not wish to emphasize the necessity of work in quite the same way. Since many people may indeed be superfluous to organized economic production, the fact of widespread unemployment might have led Miller to ask whether the unemployed can find genuine human fulfillment simply in rest.

Service to humanity and response to God form the core of the ideas concerning work in a great deal of Christian tradition, including the Protestant ethic in its original form. Questions of self-discipline were also important, but secondary to the more basic issues of human good and service to God. These points are not inconsistent with Alexander Miller's views of work, but they force us to see work in a more positive theological perspective. Seen in the light of our earlier discussion of the meaning of economic good, work can be thought of in part as cooperation with God's continuing act of creation—something which will be required long after the most basic economic needs have been met.

This is a very serious ethical claim to make. What it means is that the Christian's root motivation must merge with God's. The Christian must seek to participate in creating the conditions of God's intended covenant community of mankind. His motivation cannot be narrow or selfish, any more than God's intentions are narrow or selfish. The end in view, the objective of his work, is a world more hospitable to human good as God intends it and as man, through faith and intellect, can understand it.

A Christian understanding of work is not limited to producing and rearranging the material conditions of existence. It also involves man's expression of the meaning of life. Through service to one another, we do more than deal with material conditions; we also symbolize our mutuality, our acceptance of one another, and our attempt to establish meaningful relationships. Of course, some "service" is such that relationships are undermined rather than supported, as I shall attempt to show later. But truly human service brings fulfillment to human relationships. Work creates the content of shared experience: it represents our offering to fellow human beings. In this sense, all true service and all true creativity is profoundly social.

We can digress momentarily to note that one of the profounder insights of Hegelian philosophy and of the Marxist humanist tradition is the notion that man "actualizes" his true humanity through work. Until one labors and creates something, one is only potentially human. One's creation becomes the basis for one's interaction with others, and without this interaction one cannot become truly human. Of course, this way of putting it has its dangers. We must avoid the illusion that our humanity is "self-made." Nevertheless, our humanity does find its fulfillment in this created world through our concrete, outgoing expressions. This includes the whole of man's cultural as well as his material expressions.

In a Christian frame of reference, all true creativity is also profoundly theological. It is a man's expression of his total relation to God. Great art, in this sense, is the artist's interpretation of the whole meaning of existence. But more commonplace labors can have the same theological significance. People can repair automobiles or wash dishes to the greater glory of God.

Doubtless most people do not see work in this way. I do not believe we ought to sentimentalize the meaning of work in such a way that we draw the wrong assumptions about why people work or what it means to them. For many people work doubtless means a curse. Even for those who profess to be most attached to their endeavors the real meaning may be less than human. Work can be the basis and expression of a thoroughly selfish view of life. It can cut one off from real mutuality of relationship, and it can express alienation from God. The devil, as they say, works very hard. As a matter of fact, this world might be a better place if there weren't so many people working so diligently to tear it apart!

Nevertheless, it remains true that humanizing work is work which contributes to fellow humanity and which expresses man's faith in the unity, purpose, and goodness of ultimate reality. It is this kind of work which is ethically important.

Returning to our fourfold outline of definitions of work and leisure, clearly it is the broad view of work which must be applied. Work is not just what we get paid for doing; it includes all meaningful activity. There is a place in this for "gainful employment" (depending upon how the economy is organized) and for "voluntary service." There is also a place for lonely creativity, the value of which will not immediately be recognized. The relationship between an income-producing job and this unrewarded creativity is aptly illustrated by Charles Ives, an American composer of avant-garde symphonies who was gainfully employed in the insurance business. A nineteenth-century graduate in music, Ives early decided that the "market" would not "buy" his brand of music. Rather than compromise his creative integrity, he went to work in the insurance business and did his composing on the side. While his own contemporaries did not recognize the merit of his compositions, they are only today beginning to receive wide acclaim. According to a Christian understanding of work, his most important labor surely was that of musical composition—not the business activity through which he secured enough income to do that composing. But both remunerative work and work which is not marketable can be viewed as ethically significant.

Nevertheless, the Christian must take the broad understanding of work and narrow it in a different way. He must limit work to what *is* constructive, to what *does* undergird the good of mankind and express his faithful unity with God and fellow humanity. There may be a place in this for activities which range from the sublime to the frivolous. In some sense, every man's work will be his own unique contribution. But there would seem to be no place here for slavery or "make work" arrangements. In an intriguing paper on this subject, Paul Jacobs describes some of the problems with artificially contrived labor which has little meaning beyond just keeping people busy.[5] His illustrations drawn from the printing industry are particularly striking. Sometimes, in order to keep the work force occupied, foremen have assigned their men the task of making up pages of print—only to see them broken down again after the long hours of effort. This is similar to the proverbial stories of WPA workers during the Depression who had to dig ditches which other crews of workers would immediately fill up. Aside from the dubious element of "self-discipline" involved in such work, it is difficult to see how it has positive moral significance. It is much more likely to be dehumanizing, for it involves treating human beings as if they were things. When we describe work as a humanly necessary thing, we do not mean work which merely turns us into machines for no purpose.[6]

What, then, should we say about leisure? It has always been understood, even by the sternest interpreters of the "Protestant ethic," that man must have *some* free time. Periods of activity must alternate with periods of rest and renewal, and gainful employment must be supplemented with other forms of activity. Even complete idleness is periodically necessary. But a life of complete idleness is depressing, as many people have discovered to their astonishment. The golden dream of retirement often turns to ashes, as empty days follow in endless procession and life becomes a senseless burden. Of course many other people have found it possible to make better use of retirement. For them, it has opened up new vistas of freedom, creativity, and service. These people can provide us with a better model of approach to leisure. Meaningful activity is not limited to a traditional job. We can be grateful if increasingly we shall be liberated from routines of labor so that our activity can be more creative and free.

Which People Are "Deserving"?

If there is any typical complaint about public welfare programs, it must be the feeling that they involve "hand-outs" to people who

[5] Paul Jacobs, *Dead Horse and the Featherbird* (Santa Barbara, Calif.: Center for the Study of Democratic Institutions, 1962).

[6] For some thoughtful reflections on this point, see Michael D. Reagan, "For a Guaranteed Income," *The New York Times Magazine* (June 7, 1964). Reagan writes that "to the objection that work and self-respect are inseparable, the major reply is that the real necessity is not for a production job, but for meaningful activity. This may or may not be related to income."

don't deserve them. Our inherited economic ethic insists that people should only get what they deserve, and this means that they must work for it. It is, indeed, widely believed that there is a connection between poverty and lack of character and, vice versa, that wealth and affluence come mainly to those who are deserving. The nineteenth-century Episcopalian Bishop William Lawrence said it well in his famous remark that "in the long run, it is only to the man of morality that wealth comes. . . . Godliness is in league with riches."

Andrew Carnegie, one of the most visionary and sensitive of the tycoons of the last century, applied this philosophy directly to the question of aid to the poor: "Those worthy of assistance, except in rare cases, seldom require assistance. The really valuable men of the race never do, except in cases of accident or sudden change." Carnegie went on to say that we should be even more careful not to aid the unworthy than we are to aid the deserving, "for in alms-giving more injury is probably done by rewarding vice than relieving virtue." "It were better for mankind," he insisted, "that the millions of the rich were thrown into the sea than so spent as to encourage the slothful, the drunken, the unworthy."

This attitude is to some degree still with us. It shadows the guaranteed income question and raises nagging doubts about the moral wisdom of providing income without work.

But this attitude nevertheless runs afoul of a central Christian teaching: namely, that *no* man ought to consider himself to be "worthy" or "deserving." Every man should be more realistic and humble about his own sinfulness, for all of us are self-centered to some degree. The less aware we are of our own sinfulness the more likely it is that we are completely self-centered. For all this talk about a "Protestant ethic," the old Puritan reformers understood this well. They emphasized that, if it is a matter of deserving, what we all deserve is to burn in Hell! We need only recall such sermonic gems as Jonathan Edwards' "Sinners in the Hands of an Angry God" to put to rest the notion that the early Protestants considered godliness to be in league with riches, or any such thing. In this respect they were in harmony with Christian scripture and tradition. Jesus himself reserved his most biting and sarcastic criticism for the self-righteous who presumed to judge themselves superior to their fellows in the sight of God.

66

The positive side of this Christian awareness of man's sinfulness is the conviction that by God's gifts of creation and grace we are *given* the opportunity of life. This created possibility of life is given *prior* to questions of deserving: God "makes his sun rise on the evil and on the good, and sends rain on the just and on the unjust" (Matthew 5:45). Significantly, Jesus offered this as a reason why his followers ought not to decide whether to do good to others on the basis of their deserving it. We must do good to others, whether or not we think they deserve it—just as God's love is prior to our deserving. As this has been put, somewhat inelegantly, God holds us in his hands even while we spit in his eye. He guarantees us the ground to stand upon, even though we may use the sacred opportunity of life for evil ends. He has given us the freedom and the material preconditions necessary to do evil—otherwise we would not have the freedom and material preconditions necessary to do good.

Underlying all this there is a quite basic, but very important point: if we have to earn life and love, then what we *do* is more important than what we already *are*. In Christian teaching, what we are is children of God, and this quite overshadows the question of what we do. In fact, the lack of security in the awareness of our belonging to God is responsible for our most frantic efforts to thrust ourselves forward at the expense of our fellows. Life in a normal human family provides us with a good illustration. Where children are deeply valued by their parents, what the children are is much more important than what they do. A child's behavior may cause his parents no end of distress and embarrassment, but the parent's love is more fundamental than this behavior. Only in this kind of security is real moral growth possible. Children who are insecure in the love of their parents may learn to perform well, but the reason for their performance will likely be fear rather than their desire to do good for the sake of the good.

In this theological perspective, the Warner-Swasey advertisement (which was quoted in Chapter II) is startlingly contrary to the Christian faith. Note in particular the line, "we had self-respect, because whatever we had, however little it was, *we earned.*" Putting aside the rank individualism of the whole message, notice the pathetic self-centeredness of this "whatever we had . . . we earned." Did "we earn" the gift of life itself? Did "we

67

earn" the nurturing love of parents? Did "we earn" the physical world with its abundant resources? Did "we earn" the inheritance of thousands of years of civilization, the art and invention of millions of cooperating hands before our birth? Did "we earn" God's love, and the promise that our little lives should find meaning and purpose in relationship to the whole of being? Christian faith and honest realism alike compel us to remember that we earn little and that we may deserve less.

A companion part of Christian teaching is the warning against judging other people. We are told to "judge not, lest ye too be judged." We are reminded that judgment finally is in God's hands, for God alone can see into the human heart. Jesus' little story about the Pharisee and the publican praying in the temple makes the point. The self-righteous Pharisee thanks God loudly that he, the Pharisee, is not like other men. The publican (tax collector—generally hated in Jesus' time) on the other hand beats his breast and says, "God, be merciful to me a sinner!" Jesus makes clear that it is the publican who is actually closer to God.

Practically speaking, of course, it is very difficult to judge others anyway. Who really knows enough of the relevant background facts? Who knows another person's real capacities or his real intentions? Who is aware of the kinds of temptations against which another person must struggle? And more to the point, who ever judges himself as thoroughly as he judges others?

There is another New Testament parable which is so directly to the point of this discussion that one wonders whether it might not have been spoken with twentieth-century economic attitudes in mind! This is the parable of the vineyard (Matthew 20:1-16). According to this intriguing story, a householder hired a group of laborers to spend the day picking his grapes. He agreed to pay them a denarius for the work. Later in the day, at various times, he hired still other workers to pick grapes. Finally, just an hour before quitting time, he hired even more workers. Then, when it was time to pay the workers, the employer paid them all precisely the same wage, one denarius. This, understandably, made those who had worked all day quite furious. But the householder insisted that it was his right to pay what he wished and that he had not cheated anybody.

In this story, the "wage" is unrelated to the amount of "work."

The question whether those who were hired last deserved as much remuneration as those who had picked grapes all day did not enter into the employer's judgment.

New Testament scholars generally agree that this story is more designed to illustrate Jesus' teaching concerning divine grace than it is to spell out a theory of wages. Nevertheless, this only emphasizes all the more that God's gifts are given without respect to deserving, and that they are equally available to all his children. The emphasis is upon God's generosity, not upon man's deserving.

The whole question of who is and who is not deserving may thus be the Achilles heel of the "Protestant ethic" as we have inherited it. There is no basis in Christian ethics for human decisions as to which of our fellowmen deserve and which do not deserve the material conditions necessary for life in human community.

But how, then, should we view the relationship between God's good gifts and man's active response? To say that God's creation and grace are provided for undeserving sinners does not mean that it does not matter whether or how we respond. What we *do* is important. If it were not, then the very concept of ethics would be meaningless. But it makes a difference whether or not we view ethics as a matter of *response*. When man has freedom to respond or not to respond, then ethics becomes a meaningful subject. But ethics, apart from freedom, is a form of slavery. This can become clearer if we consider it in relation to the question of motivation and incentive, a question which is also at the root of the guaranteed income debate.

The Question of Incentives

The word incentive may be defined as a specific inducement to behave in a particular kind of way.[7] The question of incentives is involved in guaranteed income whenever people ask whether an assured income without work would undermine the desire to work. It raises both practical and moral issues. *Why* we do what we

[7] Incentive, therefore, presupposes the existence of basic drives or motives which are more fundamental. For an excellent discussion of the economic meaning of incentives and motives, see Walter G. Muelder, *Religion and Economic Responsibility* (New York: Scribner's, 1953), pp. 78-89.

do is clearly an ethical and religious matter, whatever we may also wish to say about practical considerations. The means we use to influence the behavior of others also raise religious and ethical questions.

Two distinctions will help us to understand what is at stake in a Christian approach to incentives.

The first is the distinction between positive and negative incentives. A *positive* incentive is an inducement to act in a certain way because we want something—the "carrot" approach. A *negative* incentive is an inducement to behave in a certain way because we want to avoid some undesirable consequence—the "stick" approach. A boy may be promised an increase in his allowance if he mows the lawn, or he may be threatened with a whipping if he does not. The first would be a positive incentive, the second negative. Both positive and negative incentives are involved in present-day inducements to work. The wages we wish to earn could be considered a positive incentive, while the social stigma associated with idleness is negative. Most present-day public welfare programs involve both: the financial grants are a positive incentive, but the stigma involved in being a welfare recipient is a negative one. The positive and the negative, in this case, are in conflict with each other. Presumably the negative incentive acts as a curb on the positive, so that many people will not wish to go on the welfare rolls even though they may need to, and so that those who do accept welfare aid will wish to get off the rolls as soon as possible.

Which is more "Christian"? From the biblical point of view, there is some place for both the positive and negative in human motivation. But it is an important Christian insight that man's *ultimate* motivation ought to be and can be positive. In response to God's good gifts of creation and grace, man is free to seek the good *for the sake of the good.* Man need no longer be driven by anxiety and fear of the evil to be avoided in his actions. He has an ultimate security in the knowledge that he is a child of God, and that what he is is more important to God than what he does. Therefore, he is free to act in grateful response to what God has already done for him. According to Paul, who emphasized this teaching most among the early Christians, Christ has set us free from religious laws. Religious law is essentially negative; it teaches

70

us what to avoid, and we keep the law in order to escape the consequences of our not keeping it. It is a slavedriver and a curse. In Paul's understanding, Christ has set us free by revealing to us that we are not God's slaves but God's sons and heirs. The negativism of law is replaced by a living, positive reality—when we are motivated by this reality, not by the negative law.

But there is also a place for the negative. Generally speaking, its place is to keep us out of trouble prior to our realization of our responsible freedom in God. It also helps us to identify points where our behavior will have destructive consequences. Negative law can help us even when we recognize that our ultimate security lies in our faith in God. It can point to specific, objective pitfalls which need to be avoided—not for the sake of making ourselves acceptable to God, but for the sake of the good we hope to achieve for its own sake. Thus, when we speak of the ultimate basis of motivation in Christian life, it is positive; although, relatively speaking, there is still a valid place for the negative. This leads us to the other distinction.

This is the distinction between relative and absolute incentives. A relative incentive is one which rewards or punishes behavior within the social system but which does not call into question the person's continued membership in the community. The reward is *relatively* desirable, the punishment is *relatively* undesirable. It is assumed that the reward or punishment will be sought or avoided when offered as an alternative to antisocial or social behavior. Normal parental discipline is a good illustration. While a child may be given some little reward for his behavior, and while he may be punished (even spanked) for bad behavior, there is never any question about his continuing to be a member of the family.

An *absolute* incentive, on the other hand, is based on making one's continued membership in the community into a reward or punishment. One's social existence itself is thus at stake in one's actions. The best illustration of this is capital punishment. The negative incentive used to deter people from murder is the threat of execution, and it is presumed that people will avoid behavior which will result in their own extinction. An absolute incentive is also implied in the behavior of parents who disown their own children—such as the mother I once overheard in a juvenile court

71

telling her delinquent son that, so far as she was concerned, he was no longer her son. She thus informed her son that the reason why he ought not to have behaved as he had was that he would thereby remove himself from membership in the family. Doubtless many children are made to *feel* that they will not be accepted by their parents unless they behave in prescribed ways, although the matter is rarely put in such direct language.

As we have seen, Christian teaching about God emphasizes that our being children of God (or being "saved") is not dependent upon what we do or do not do—hence that God does not use salvation as an incentive for our good behavior. Grace is prior to works. What we do in the way of good works is in response to what God has already done; it is not because God has laid an absolute incentive over our heads. Similarly, through creation we are given the opportunity of physical existence. We are given the ground to stand upon. Our physical existence itself is not made into an incentive for our good behavior, although we can despoil this inheritance so as to destroy it for ourselves. We are given a security through grace and through creation which relativizes questions of incentives. To put this in a somewhat different way, God, through creation and grace, grants us the full opportunity to fulfill our destiny in response to him. Opportunity in this sense is a preincentive. It must be secure for incentive itself to have any meaning.

On this basis, should we not avoid manipulating the lives of people by calling their very social existence into question? If, in their actions, people feel that they must constantly be on the defensive, they are hardly free to respond creatively; they are not at liberty to seek the good for the sake of the good itself. I recall a soup kitchen which was maintained by a gospel mission in a California city. The food was free. But prior to their supper the skid row derelicts were required to attend church. Since they absolutely depended upon the handout, services were well attended indeed! As a matter of fact, "sincere" professions of faith and conversion were quite frequent. But one always wondered whether it was the gospel or the empty stomach. Is the gospel so weak that its appeal must be supplemented by the threat of hunger—just in case?

If we desire truly *moral* motivation, must we not first help secure people in their existence as human beings? Did not Jesus

72

heal and feed before preaching? Did he not do so as a matter of securing people in their physical existence, and not as a matter of incentive?

Some have ventured even to argue that the best way to motivate people to work is first to guarantee them their basic material security. Economist Clarence E. Ayres believes that

security is the key to the enigma of poverty, as it was to the impasse of feudal serfdom. With the guarantee of a subsistence income, so that come what may they could feel assured that they would not starve to death, most of the present victims of poverty would make the effort of reorienting themselves to the industrial economy.[8]

Psychologist Erich Fromm contrasts a psychology of scarcity, which "produces anxiety, envy, egotism," with a psychology of abundance, which "produces initiative, faith in life, solidarity." [9] Relating this to freedom, Fromm holds that guaranteed income could

for the first time free man from the threat of starvation, and thus make him truly free and independent from any economic threat. . . . It would also establish a principle deeply rooted in Western religious and humanist tradition: man has the right to live, regardless! This right to live, to have food, shelter, medical care, education, etc., is an intrinsic human right that cannot be restricted by any condition, not even the one that he must be socially "useful."

Such statements are not necessarily inconsistent with *relative* incentives. Once the absolute conditions of man's physical and social existence have been assured, then relative inducements of one sort or another may (or may not) make sense depending upon the circumstances. To illustrate, many of us unfortunately need a relative negative incentive to help regulate our driving habits. We might be inclined to fudge a bit on the speed limit if we did not have policemen on hand to remind us of our responsibilities on the highway. The legal penalty for infractions is a relative one. The penalty does not in itself call our social existence into

[8] "Guaranteed Income: An Institutionalist View," in Robert Theobald, ed., *The Guaranteed Income*, p. 176.

[9] "The Psychological Aspects of the Guaranteed Income," in *ibid.*, p. 184.

question (although our driving habits might!). But it is painful enough to make us think twice. Similarly, it may be that certain relative economic incentives are necessary to get people to produce actively enough to supply the objective needs. The guaranteed income concept does not rule this possibility out, although it is inconsistent with use of economic gain as an absolute incentive.

Some systems of reward and punishment may be socially necessary in order to control the negative effects of man's self-centered, antisocial tendencies. We cannot assume that everybody will be motivated to act responsibly without relative incentives. As Martin Luther once put the dilemma, "Take heed and first fill the world with real Christians before you attempt to rule it in a Christian and evangelical manner." Luther doubted that this could be done, and he wished to protect society from the results of human sinfulness.

We should also remember that deliberate attempts to create incentives may risk the loss of creativity by encouraging people to seek rewards which are different from the goals logically related to one's actions. When we refrain from speeding only because we risk arrest and some embarrassment, we substitute that incentive for the more rational goal of safety. The use of grading in schools and colleges is another illustration. Where grades are used as incentives, there is some risk that students will work for the grades instead of working for knowledge or in order to prepare themselves to deal with the future. Nevertheless, such incentive systems may sometimes be a relative necessity. We should not rule them out altogether, provided they are relative and not absolute.

Before leaving the subject of incentives, we must not overlook some mention of the motives which we do well *not* to appeal to in our efforts to induce people to exert themselves.

Materialism is clearly one such form of motivation. Where material things are made into ultimate values, where we become attached to them as intrinsic and not simply instrumental values, there something has gone wrong. The meeting of material need and the creation of material comforts and conveniences is a valid human desire. But such things cannot become the sum and substance of human life without undercutting man's true nature. Doubtless we need to challenge the massive elements of materialism in our culture more vigorously than we have done in the past.

74

But I wish to speak even more sharply at another point which may represent a greater danger because it is less obvious. This is the use of "status-seeking" as a basic incentive. If the reward which we use as an incentive is a higher status relative to fellow human beings, then it is a symbol of separation. Conscious effort to be superior to our fellows at the least isolates us from them spiritually. The ironic reward for our character and industriousness can thus be our spiritual isolation. We are paid for our superior contribution by being deprived of that community with our fellow-man through which alone we can find fulfillment.

The system of status and status-seeking in our society is so pervasive that most of us take it entirely for granted. It is a part of "our way of life," although when we begin to define life in terms of status it takes us away from a Christian understanding. An excellent illustration of how far we go to use status-seeking as an incentive is provided by a study which was made of the social structure of a New York corporation. This corporation had moved its management staff into a new building where the offices were designed so as to reflect the appropriate status of their occupants. The president had an office suite with paneled walls, wall-to-wall carpeting, and various other symbols. Vice-presidents had wall-to-wall carpeting and some, but not all, of the other perquisites, And so on down the line. By accident it was discovered that one of the junior executives had been given an office with wall-to-wall carpeting when he was supposed to rate only an ordinary rug. So workmen were sent in to cut a fringe around the edge of the wall-to-wall carpet! This may not be a bad parable of our civilization. But we are not sensitive enough to see that whatever it is that separates us from our fellow human beings also separates us from our own true humanity.

This destructive form of reward may be mitigated in part when the economic gain can be passed on to the family—as when a man seeks the incentive reward for the sake of his family. The family, as a unit of fellow humanity, is intrinsic—not instrumental. Nevertheless, as Reinhold Niebuhr and others have shown, when the family itself is set apart from the rest of the community (or when any other group is set apart from the rest of the total society), it also becomes in itself a structure of human alienation. All members of the family thus share, to some extent, in the alienated existence.

75

This may be one reason why the children of privileged families occasionally throw off their privileges and seek to identify themselves more directly with the rest of society.

The tendency of economic and social incentives, when placed in an individualistic form, is to transform the instrumental function of economic life into an intrinsic end. More precisely, the tendency is for economic life, which should be the basis or external condition of fulfillment in "covenant community," to become exactly the opposite. The tendency is for it to become a barrier to the fulfillment of life. The true ends of human life are subordinated to the less than human.

The Expectation of Gratitude

One of the striking aspects of most welfare programs, whether public or private, is the expectation that the recipient will humbly acknowledge his indebtedness and properly express his gratitude to the giver. The outraged public response to the Welfare Rights Movement was revealing. More than anything else, the members of this movement (mostly mothers on welfare) sought to have their aid payments considered as a basic right, not as a gift. But most other people are accustomed to thinking of anything which is not earned through work as a gift, and it is believed that the recipients should be grateful to the givers.

In a Christian perspective, something can be said for the viewpoint of the apparently ungrateful welfare mothers. If one accepts the idea that creation is given to all of us alike (and apart from our deserving), it is clear that when social provision is made for basic economic well-being the gratitude belongs not so much to other people as to our Creator.

Misplaced gratitude can create the notion that the receiver is somehow inferior to the giver (unless, of course, it is a truly shared experience with mutual giving, mutual gratitude, and mutual respect). Gratitude can therefore lead also to human separation. I am afraid that some of the "warm feeling" which accompanies much of our giving is not so much the inner glow of Christian radiance as it is the pride which comes from playing God and the assuaged conscience which is prematurely content with problems only half-solved. The symbolic Christmas basket has generally made us all feel better. But it leaves the humiliated poor in a scarcely improved condition. There is much to be said for an objective handling of the basic conditions of life, treating them rather as a basic human right for which grateful thanks belong, not to any human agency, but to God alone.

Something is particularly wrong with the use of material giving in order to manipulate the response of others. Years ago we used to speak of the "rice Christians": persons who became Christians in countries like China in order to get more rice. Doubtless they were volubly grateful. It is less certain whether they were very dedicated Christians. And the worst of it was that one could never be sure!

Let there be no misunderstanding at this point. People ought to be grateful. Apart from gratitude we become arrogant and contemptuous of our good gifts. But when gratitude must take the form of being thankful to other men for the conditions of life itself, then the Christian must say that that kind of gratitude belongs rather to God.

Some Conclusions

How should we summarize this discussion? The most important point to remember is that the basic conditions of human existence ought to be secured prior to all talk about earning or deserving or incentive. The whole point of economics is to create and maintain the material conditions which best *serve* man's true humanity. When the latter is subordinated to the former, when man's integrity and his social relationships are turned into instruments of production, then economic life destroys rather than fulfills our spiritual destiny. To the Christian, as we have seen, this must be understood in terms of God's acts of creation and grace. Through these acts, man has been given freedom and the ground to stand upon. Christian response to what God has done involves gratitude and creative service. It involves the attempt to cooperate with God so as to fashion a world more and more hospitable to the covenant community of mankind which is God's intention. Christian response does not involve the withholding of the necessary conditions of life as a means of manipulating the spiritual life of one's fellows.

Whatever one may say concerning the importance of work (and I consider work to be necessary to man's personal and social fulfillment), it loses its Christian significance when it is slavery or when it is an anxious attempt to make oneself worthy. It contributes to genuine fulfillment instead when it is an attempt to do the good or necessary thing because it is good or necessary, as one's free gift in response to God and in love of one's fellow creatures.

In this perspective, the "Protestant ethic" (which as we have received it may be a distortion of both ethics and of Protestantism) represents a half-truth. The true half is the importance of work in human fulfillment. The false half is the subordination of man to work and, worse yet, the attempt to establish whether or not people are deserving of what God has already given them.

We must reject even more emphatically the gross materialism and individualism of many of our inherited economic attitudes. Man was not made for material ends; nor can we limit human creativity to what will bring cash in the marketplace. Any definition of man's nature which treats him as an isolated stranger among his fellows destroys his true humanity just as surely as does any totalitarian effort to dissolve his uniqueness in social conformity. Man is both personal and social by nature.

These perspectives should have much to say to us about such proposals as guaranteed income.

Chapter IV

CHRISTIAN SUPPORT FOR GUARANTEED INCOME

The issue before us is now a rather simple one. Should we or should we not guarantee the basic material conditions of human life as a social right of every man? We can put aside the questions of practical detail long enough to answer yes or no to that one question.

On the basis of the preceding chapter, the moral answer can be an emphatic *yes.* Objections to "income without work" may have *some* validity at the level of "relative incentives," but they have none whatsoever at the level of "absolute incentives." Man's right to be—his right to physical and social existence—is not something for his fellowmen to grant or withhold as an economic inducement or give as a gift. We should be happy instead that present levels of productivity and material abundance make it possible to translate this moral judgment into economic reality, and thus further to undergird human community and freedom. Guaranteed income as a secure economic floor will make it possible for men to become what God intended them to become by free response. The fact that many will doubtless abuse this freedom is a risk which God has taken in creating man in the first place. We need not feel that it is a risk which we take upon ourselves. We are relieved of the intolerable burden of having to decide which ones among our fellows do and do not deserve an economic floor to stand upon. In one sense *none* of us deserve this right. But in a deeper sense, this right to be is one which God has given to each of us regardless of our undeserving. Guaranteed income will be a recognition, in economic terms, of what God has done.

We have long since grown accustomed to this in relation to our own families. When our children are born, none of us ask whether or not they deserve the food, clothing, shelter, and care which they need in order to survive. For at least the first few years, no question of "earning" comes into the picture. Often it begins to be raised in connection with a child's allowance or special privileges. But, with rare exceptions, most of us treat the whole question of incentives for our children as a quite relative thing. They don't have to earn the basics. We hope they will be grateful, but sometimes they are not. Nevertheless, good parents do not disown their children. At this basic level there is guaranteed security.

But is guaranteed income for some (a minority of the people) equitable to the rest? I am not sure how important this question is, but we must not forget that guaranteed income is security for *everybody,* even though it has to be used by only a few. In this sense it is like insurance protection. It benefits us by providing us with the assurance that adversity will not be a total disaster to ourselves or our survivors. It should make all of us breathe a bit easier. If the worst should come to the worst, economically, we will still be able to keep our head above water. We will also be a bit freer from social conformity if our economic circumstances cannot be used to control us. Furthermore, security for our fellows is also security for us in our relationship with them. Guaranteed income helps protect all of us from the kinds of income disparities which undermine human fellowship. Since rich and poor alike are diminished by their spiritual insulation from each other, economic security for the poor will provide a kind of spiritual security for the rich.

Having recorded an emphatic *yes* to the basic question of whether or not we should support guaranteed income, the various specific proposals still need to be subjected to careful scrutiny. They need to be looked at both ethically and practically. In a small volume such as this, it is not possible to provide the full analysis needed. Besides, different kinds of specialists need to help us sort out the technical details of any program as wide-ranging as guaranteed income.

Nevertheless, I wish to make a few comments on ethical issues raised by the different proposals which were outlined in the first chapter. This may help suggest some of the lines which further discussion might follow. It is possible to note both positive and negative elements in most of the different proposals. It is possible to say "yes," "no," and "maybe" in order to indicate points of acceptance, points of rejection, and points which need further study and thought.

Robert Theobald's "Basic Economic Security"

We can say *yes* to Theobald's central concept that economic security can and ought now to be guaranteed as a basic human right. Of all the major voices in the debate over guaranteed income, Theobald seems to have the surest sense of this moral issue and its social consequences. Our rapidly increasing abundance will become a curse if we do not use it instead to undergird everyone's social dignity. Moreover, Theobald is insistent that the size of the income grants be large enough actually to lift people above the poverty level. He also believes that provision should be made for continued increases to reflect the increasing general productivity and affluence of society. To these points we can also say yes.

If we need to criticize Theobald, it is probably at the point of his lack of attention to the problem of providing sufficient stimulation and channels for creative outlet. He rather seems to assume that the poor, when liberated from their insecurity and drugery, will blossom forth with poetry, the arts, and crafts of all sorts. Doubtless this is a half-truth, and we must not dismiss Theobald's optimistic doctrine of man too lightly. But particularly among the culturally deprived we cannot realistically expect everybody to be a self-starter. Theobald cannot be accused of advocating idleness or passivity. But his basic proposals could be improved by including structured provision for work opportunity.

At several points we can also say *maybe*. For example, Theobald's unconcern over the use of incentive features in Basic Economic Security is based on his assumption that at that level incentive is unnecessary—either so far as the individual is concerned or for the sake of total production. He may be right; but enough economists disagree with him to raise doubts among thoughtful laymen. Before totally dispensing with *relative* economic incentives, this kind of question needs more careful study. Or, to take another of his ideas, Theobald's proposed income maintenance plan for the middle-income categories ought also to be studied more closely. This idea of "committed spending" does commend itself from the standpoint of the social stability of middle-income people who are also vulnerable to technological change. But it may raise questions of equity, and it ought also to be studied in terms of its effects upon incentive. In any event, the "committed spending" proposal is not essential to guaranteed income, nor is Theobald's general attitude toward incentives. His views should help keep the economic effects of cybernation and automation before us. As we gain more experience it may become clearer whether the new productive forces will be as radical in their effects upon employment as he believes they will be.

Theobald's "consentive" idea (non-profit productive organizations whose members consent to work together while receiving guaranteed income) would not require special action once guaranteed income became a reality, but it is the kind of thing which society might well encourage.

Milton Friedman's Negative Income Tax Proposal

The "negative income tax" idea has been suggested with many variations by numerous economists. As a general idea, it is not necessarily different from Theobald's Basic Economic Security, although most of the economists who favor negative income taxes are much more concerned about incentives. Milton Friedman's views merit special comment, both because of their uniqueness and because of his conservatism.

From an ethical standpoint, we can say *yes* to Friedman's concern for moral integrity and respect for the dignity of welfare recipients. He conveys real understanding of the relationship between a basic minimum of economic security and the political freedom which he values so highly. He is properly critical of the demeaning paternalism of much public relief. He wishes to give the poor the human dignity which can only come through objective standards to establish need and through granting the poor the freedom to use their resources as they see fit.

But we must be less enthusiastic about other features of Friedman's approach. While guaranteed income might well make it possible for us to dispense with a lot of the present welfare apparatus (more on this later), it would be sheer madness to think of this kind of basic economic security as a substitute for *all* welfare programs. Programs of an educational nature (including job training, advice to homemakers, family counseling, etc.) will still be needed. In fact, such services ought to be more valuable when they can be separated from income-granting responsibilities. Similarly, such services as children's homes and adoption agencies cannot simply be left to private initiative, and many of the public programs for the elderly may still be required. Moreover, I hope we will be much more generous in the minimum amounts of grants than Friedman seems to be suggesting. To establish a poverty-line figure and then set the basic grant at only half that amount seems a curious way to fight poverty! As long as the society can afford it—which Friedman himself does not doubt—why not make the size of the grant at least the amount needed to lift people above the poverty line? Friedman's answer is that this might destroy incentive. But if the incentive is itself a part of one's basic minimum level of subsistence, it is more an absolute than a relative incentive. It is therefore subject to the criticisms introduced in Chapter III.

There are also a couple of "maybes" about Friedman's proposals. The question of exactly how much incentive we need is one of these. So is the question of exactly how many of our present programs we could dismantle if we were to adopt the negative tax. In the long run, we may also have to say "maybe" about the free market, which is so important to Friedman. Many aspects of the free market are doubtless good. It is one of the best ways of fitting production to the real wants of people, it encourages free creativity in invention and marketing, and it is a good way to establish relative costs and prices. But Friedman may be a little naïve about just how "free" the free market can be in a mass society, at least so far as certain products are concerned. Mass manipulation through advertising and administered prices in certain industries greatly limits this nineteenth-century vision of competitive free enterprise. I put this down as a "maybe" because any changes in the market system should doubtless be handled on a pragmatic basis over a long period of time. But we should be reluctant to join Friedman in an absolute ideological commitment to what may turn out to be partly an illusion.

The Social Dividend

This idea is not different in essence from the foregoing, so long as it is combined with the present progressive income tax system. Nevertheless, one aspect of the justification or rationale of the "social dividend" needs to be challenged on moral grounds. That is the idea that if the public makes any grants it ought necessarily to make them equally to all citizens, rich and poor alike. For one thing, the prosperous already receive social benefits of a hundred direct and indirect kinds which are denied to the poor. Most governmental grants and subsidies go to the "haves" rather than the "have-nots," a point which we constantly overlook in criticizing welfare programs. But more importantly, guaranteed income does provide everybody with the same security whether or not everybody has to make use of it. It also stimulates the economy for everybody and helps to break down social barriers which invariably result from serious deprivation.

Family Allowances

The *yes* to family allowances is the particular emphasis it places upon the moral claim of children. As I shall suggest in the following chapter, the case for guaranteed income is certainly strongest in relation to children. But there are also other groups of people who need this basic security, including the aged and the handicapped or otherwise unemployable. If we really accept the idea of a basic economic security, then we have to say *no* to the limitation. We also have to say *no* to the limited size of the grants envisaged by most of those advocating the family grants approach. The sum of $8 or $12 per child per month is not enough to lift children or families out of poverty.

In devising any particular guaranteed income program there are a lot of "maybes" involved in decisions about amounts to be given for dependents in different family sizes. Some may fear that too generous amounts may accelerate the population explosion too much (although the experience of countries which have actually tried to increase their populations through family allowances is that it does not have this effect). Others may wish to deal adequately with the actual need of all children and rely upon other kinds of measures to encourage population limitation.

Guaranteed Income "in Kind"

The idea that guaranteed income should be in the form of the material necessities themselves (instead of money) is *not* one of the important options. It is worth comment, however; not just because Erich Fromm has developed some interesting ideas along this line, but also because some goods and services might be treated in this way *in addition to* basic cash grants. As a *substitute* for a guaranteed income in money, we would have to say no, at least at the present time. In a money economy (with a market based upon money), it would indeed create a separate class of people if the poor were denied purchasing power available to others. The social significance of the form of the grant could, in that case, be ethically disastrous. If the moral purpose of the economy is to provide the material basis of man's personal and communal life, this would certainly help to destroy the communal part whatever it did for the personal.

However, we can be receptive to the possibility that some services might be "in kind." We already treat public education, parks, highways, etc. very largely in this way. We may also wish to consider some aspects of medical care in the same way. This is one of those "maybe" points.

Guaranteed Opportunity to Earn an Income

There are some who are sympathetic to guaranteed income proposals but would prefer to base this upon work opportunities. Every "guaranteed opportunity" proposal needs to be scrutinized

85

with care. Often such programs do not really mean *guaranteed* opportunity. But there are those who support the idea of government as employer of last resort, and this implies a full commitment by society to provide a job for everybody who needs and wants one.

Guaranteed opportunity to work could be supported ethically, provided that this means guaranteed opportunity to earn enough income to live with decency as a member of society. It would certainly be a vast improvement over present practice, because it would be based upon *universality* of income opportunity and *adequacy* of income. But there are many "ifs" in such an approach, even beyond the question whether we really would extend this opportunity to *everybody* and the question whether we really could assure adequate compensation for the jobs thus provided.

In the first place, there is the question of those who are unable to work. Will they continue to be treated on a demeaning, paternalistic basis as though they were not equally to be regarded as human beings by their fellows? In the second place, there is the question of what forms of work will be considered worthy for inclusion in a universal work opportunity program. Will there be an implicitly narrow definition of work, or will it be keyed to the broad definition of work discussed in Chapter III? This question would have to be faced particularly with the present-day "welfare mothers." Would it be felt that being a mother is itself a worthy contribution to society? Or would such a program assume that mothers without husbands ought to have *additional* jobs? In the third place, there is the question of relative and absolute incentives. Does guaranteed work opportunity assume that the absolute economic conditions of human existence ought to be earned—and if so, why? And does it assume that it would not be possible to combine an effective relative incentive with a guaranteed basic income which could be separated from the question of work altogether? (Why not, in other words, treat man's basic economic existence as a question of right, and *then* provide incentives to work to gain more?) In the fourth place, there is the question of the difference between income based upon need and income based upon work. Two people can be employed doing the same thing. If one of them has a family of six, while the other is unmarried, the income requirements of the two will of course be vastly different. But if income is geared to work alone, the question of need will be bypassed. If (in the jobs which are provided as "last resort") wages are geared to the support of single persons, then the family of six will be grossly neglected. If, on the other hand, the wage is geared for a large family, then the single worker will be grossly overpaid! Has the guaranteed opportunity to work idea really taken into account the root question posed by guaranteed income, namely, how are we to use our affluence to insure the basic conditions of economic life to all?

In addition to such questions, it may well be asked whether we really need to force everybody to work in this way. Wouldn't it be better to take advantage of our new affluence and begin to liberate people from this necessity, now that it is economically possible to do so? Or, from a totally different perspective, others might ask what effect the guaranteed work opportunity program would have on the private sector of the economy. What would it do to the lowest paying jobs in industry? And if (as Representative Thomas Curtis and others propose) subsidies are paid to private enterprise in order to provide more jobs, what protection is there from the possibility of employers underpaying their employees and expecting government to make up the balance between their low pay and a decent minimum income?

In balance, I believe that the guaranteed opportunity idea, taken by itself, neglects some of the key points discussed in Chapter III. As I shall attempt to say in a later chapter, however, the idea may have some real merit as a *supplement* to guaranteed income.

Categorical Assistance

Categorical assistance for the most part is what we already have. It involves giving public financial grants on the basis of certain categories (such as the aged, the blind, the handicapped, etc.). Family grants would represent a kind of categorical assistance program, although there are many categories of need in addition to children. Categorical assistance could be called guaranteed income only if minimum levels of income *within* the specified categories of need were treated as a matter of absolute social right, and not as something to be determined by somebody's arbitrary judgment.

Helen O. Nicol and others who wish to improve our present programs rather than turn to one of the broader guaranteed income plans argue that this is the only way we can be sensitive to the real needs. The greater flexibility of response to a broad range of categories of need can be seen as its main value from an ethical standpoint. But at the same time, this approach tends to be more paternalistic and less objective. It risks perpetuation of the problems in present welfare programs which we are attempting to get away from. And there is the danger that, so long as we use this approach, the gates which squeak the loudest (or the groups whose needs most readily excite public sympathy) will tend to receive disproportionate attention. Continuation of the categorical assistance method is a poor way to implement the basic concept that the material conditions of man's life in community ought to be regarded as a fundamental right.

Ethical Guidelines

Is it possible, on the basis of our discussion so far, to suggest some standards by which guaranteed income proposals might be judged? Any such ethical guidelines should not be confused with concrete proposals themselves. It is beyond the purpose of this kind of book to spell out all the practical details of so vast a possibility as guaranteed income. But it may not be beyond our scope to suggest that an ethically sensitive plan ought to include the following elements:

1. The treatment of income as a universal right. Everybody has a moral right to the material conditions of his physical existence as a human being and of his ability to participate in society as a man among his fellows.

2. The avoidance of moral judgments as to who does and who does not "deserve" the basic minimum income. None of us deserve our great inheritance as human beings, and attitudes of self-righteousness are alien to Christian humility.

3. The granting of a large enough income to overcome absolute poverty, with provision for overcoming relative poverty as well. (This standard is subject, of course, to the capacity of the economy to provide such basic grants. This is no problem in the United States, but in some other countries it certainly would be.)

4. Provision of income in the same form as that typical of the society. Since we live in a basically money economy, guaranteed income should be in money primarily. (This, of course, does not exclude basic social services and public facilities which are made available to everybody.)

5. Objective methods of administration. Determination of need should be on the basis of objective criteria and not subject to the arbitrary judgment of social caseworkers or other officials.

6. Continuing development of programs to overcome cultural deprivation. Guaranteed income cannot be considered as a substitute for educational and counseling services designed to prepare people for more meaningful participation in the life of society.

7. Provision for meaningful activity. Whether or not one considers work incentives desirable, provision of opportunity for meaningful activity cannot simply be taken for granted.

8. Provision for increases in guaranteed income amounts to correspond to increases in the total productivity of the economy. If guaranteed income remains constant despite increases in per capita income, the result will be increases in relative poverty.[1]

There are, however, still other ethical issues to which we must now turn.

---

[1] These guidelines can be compared with a similar list of criteria developed by a study group sponsored by the National Council of Churches. The study group believed that any guaranteed income program should meet the following criteria: (1) It should be available to all as a matter of right. (2) It should be adequate to maintain health and human decency. (3) It should be administered so as to maximize coverage and adjust benefits to changes in cost of living. (4) It should be developed in a manner which will respect the freedom of persons to manage their own lives, increase their power to choose their own careers, and enable them to participate in meeting personal and community needs. (5) It should be designed to afford incentive to productive activity. (6) It should be designed in such a way that existing socially desirable programs and values are conserved and enhanced.

With the exception of the fifth of these, which may accept the need for incentives too uncritically, this list also expresses the basic viewpoint of Chapter III.

Chapter V

DOES GUARANTEED INCOME MEAN EQUALITY AND "COLLECTIVISM"?

Some uninformed persons may leap to the conclusion that guaranteed income will mean "socialism" or some such thing, despite the fact that Theobald, Friedman, Tobin, Lampman, and all the other major supporters of the idea are firm believers in the free market and private enterprise.[1] Strictly speaking, "socialism" means government ownership of the means of production and distribution: the factories, commercial enterprises, utilities, and so forth. Today we have, in the United States, public ownership of some things, such as highways, mail delivery, some recreation areas, dams and hydroelectric facilities, and some utilities. But most of the means of production are in private hands. As a matter of fact, *all* economic enterprises (including those presently run by government) *could* be private without affecting the concept of guaranteed income as such in the slightest. Or, on the other hand, all economic enterprises could be run by government, and this also would not affect the question. The concept of guaranteed income simply involves a public commitment to assure every citizen that his purchasing power will not fall below a specified

[1] In fact, one of Robert Lekachman's criticisms of guaranteed income is that some proponents have overlooked the need for more expenditures in the *public*, as opposed to private, sector. See his article, "The Guaranteed Annual Income: Con," in *Christianity and Crisis* (January 24, 1966).

level. It does not commit us either to public or to private ownership of economic enterprises, nor to any particular combination of public and private. It *does* commit us to a minimum income floor for everybody.

But we ought to look at this from a different angle. Does the ethical case for guaranteed income (which we have already examined) commit us ethically to *more* than guaranteed income? Does the logic of our ethical analysis compel us to go further? If it does we should pursue the logic far enough to see where it leads. In doing so, we must never forget where our real commitments lie. If we are serious in our commitment to the Christian life, then we do not owe our ultimate allegiance to any economic arrangements. We judge economic arrangements by moral standards, not the other way around.

The Moral Presumption of Equality

The first point I wish to make is that most of the ethical statements supporting guaranteed income also support equality of income. If we view economic life in instrumental terms; if we say that human personhood and social mutuality are the intrinsic goals of man's life; and if we affirm that it is the business of the economic sphere to undergird these goals for all men as a God-given precondition—then a strong case can be made for economic equality. It may be the best way to keep economic life from becoming the intrinsic good. It may best save us from materialism and status-seeking. A person who is motivated by personal economic gain has become a slave to the material world, and his integrity is undermined. A person who desires more income than his neighbors is alienated from them spiritually; that desire itself stands as a barrier between them to undermine real mutuality.

Most of us are well aware of the effects of large disparities of income upon social relationships in our society. Few wealthy men are able to view the poor as worthy of their social attention. Few poor people are able to relate to the wealthy without a sense of inferiority. If genuine community is what we want, then equality of income would seem to be a better way to get it than the inequalities to which we are accustomed. We can add one other

91

point to this: an assured equality of income is also the best way to avoid the manipulation of persons by means of their economic need. Equality is an important condition of freedom. I think it is significant that real democracy has generally flourished best in communities which have a high degree of equality. This is largely true whether we are speaking of the democracy of the Greek city-states (excluding the slave class, of course), of the farming villages in early America, or even of primitive tribal life.

The moral desirability of equality is even more compelling from a theological perspective. God's gift of creation is a gift to the whole human family. So is the gift of God's love. Every one of us is equally valued by God, as the Bible makes abundantly clear. The parable of the vineyard, which we have already examined, even uses equality of income as an illustration of the equality of God's grace. It is not because we are alike deserving. We are treated alike because we are all equally God's children—in the ultimate sense we are equal in that we are all equally human beings. Would not equality of income better order the material gifts of creation so that God's intention in creation might better be served?

Before dismissing such views casually, a Christian ought to ask himself why the Bible and the writings of early Christian leaders so often condemn wealth. Professor Henry Clark summarizes an excellent discussion of the attitude of the Bible and the early church toward wealth and poverty in these words:

The Christian case against poverty is grounded in biblical teaching about love of neighbor as the fruit of God's love for his children, and about each person's responsibility for his brothers in the family of man. Isolated verses may be cited to imply that the poor deserve their fate because the righteous prosper, but the main thrust of the gospel as found in both the Old and the New Testaments is in the direction of deeply felt compassion and generous sharing of the blessings bestowed by God.[2]

Statements by Amos, Micah, Jeremiah, and Isaiah illustrate the

[2] Henry Clark, *The Christian Case Against Poverty* (New York: Association Press, 1965), p. 14. See esp. chapter one, "A Historical View of Poverty and Wealth," pp. 14-43.

Old Testament view. In the New Testament, the story of Zaccheus, the Sermon on the Mount, the parables of Dives and Lazarus and of the Rich Young Ruler, the description of the last judgment, the statement about the difficulty of a rich man entering the Kingdom of God, the example of the church in the early chapters of Acts, and the sayings on wealth in the Epistle of James—all indicate the spiritual peril of having more of this world's goods than one's neighbors. The view was also typically held by leaders of the early church. Ambrose, for example, rebukes the rich because "you crave possessions not so much for their utility to yourself, as because you want to exclude others from them." [3] Ambrose went so far as to say that "God commanded all things to be produced so that sustenance should be common to all, and that the earth should be a sort of common possession of all men." "Nature," he continued, "created a common right, usurpation created private right."

The church gradually changed its views on economic life; but this, really, is about the attitude with which it started.

Theological justifications of inequality often fall short of the mark. They may be based upon human attempts to determine who are and who are not deserving of economic privileges, and they may even imply an out-and-out materialistic conception of the nature of man. Medieval Christianity developed a hierarchical view of man's social and economic life. It thereby justified economic and social privileges based upon one's appointed station in life. This status structure, which appears in the works of St. Thomas Aquinas in most developed form, assumes that men are placed in their stations in life by God himself. Thus God is responsible for the economic differences between the aristocrat and the peasant. The traditional medieval view did guard the basic economic well-being of every man. It was protective of the poor as well as the rich. But the traditional hierarchical status view could not survive the breakup of the medieval world. Under the searching and sometimes scathing criticism of early capitalists and political reformers, man's freedom to change his station in life was proclaimed. The contract political theorists (notably Rousseau) also insisted upon the equality of man. Once the traditional

[3] Quoted in *ibid.*, p. 21.

theological justification of divinely appointed stations in life had been undermined, subsequent theological support for inequality has rarely seemed convincing in relation to the Christian faith. It has always seemed too much like the justification of somebody's self-interest.

An exception to this is provided by the recent continental theologian Emil Brunner. In language somewhat reminiscent of the medieval view, Brunner saw human society as a series of relationships through which persons minister to one another's needs. Through the "orders of creation," the structures of man's natural life, certain relationships of mutual service are fixed. This is illustrated by the relationship of the sexes, of parent and child, of employer and employee, of ruler and ruled. The basis of inequality of material income then is in the inequalities of function which different persons are fitted to perform. Community requires diversity.[4]

This may be considered a strong theological defence of inequality. But Brunner subordinated even this to the more basic claim of equality. We are equal in a more basic sense than we are unequal. Our inequalities are relative, but our equality before God is absolute. "The cardinal factor," he writes, "is the direct responsibility of the individual to God implied in God's call, and the dignity and equality which result from it. The secondary, though not inessential, factor is the mutual dependence resulting from man's predestination to fellowship and its substratum in nature, individual limitation and idiosyncrasy." He summarizes this view by saying that "in the Christian idea of justice, equality and the equal right of all are primary, while the difference of what is due to each in the fellowship is, though not inessential, secondary." [5]

Where does this leave us? I believe we can translate Brunner's view in economic terms in relation to our distinction between relative and absolute incentives. Christian economic policy must aim to achieve the basic (absolute) economic well-being of all persons so that their physical needs are met and so that their opportunity to participate in human society is assured. Economic

---

[4] Emil Brunner, *Justice and the Social Order*, trans. Mary Hottinger (New York: Harper & Brothers, 1945), pp. 37 ff.

[5] *Ibid.*, p. 43.

inequalities above this point might be accepted as necessary, so long as they were not large enough to undermine social relationships.

But there may be a better way to summarize the economic meaning of the Christian view that all men are equal. This is simply to say that equality is the norm or standard, and that any deviations from equality must bear the burden of proof. The moral presumption should be *for* equality and *against* inequality. Certain inequalities may indeed be necessary for the sake of life in this world as God has intended it. But, if there is any doubt, our presumption must be that the inequalities ought not to be approved.[6]

Practical and Necessary Exceptions

Are there, then, good enough reasons to support inequality of income? Can inequalities bear this burden of proof?

As a general principle, we ought to be able to show that inequalities are necessary for the sake of God's intended covenant community, and not for any other reason of convenience or self-interest. To put this differently: in justifying inequality it needs to be shown that if inequality were *not* permitted, actual conditions would have effects more damaging to the form of covenant community than if it were.

I believe there are at least five kinds of practical and necessary exceptions which can meet this test.

First, there are inequalities of income resulting from inequalities of actual physical need. In this case, an inequality is needed in

[6] The term "moral presumption" should be understood carefully. A moral presumption locates the burden of proof *for* certain norms and *against* deviations. We presume that a moral norm ought to be applied as directly as possible. Certain deviations may be necessary for moral reasons. But the deviations bear the burden of proof. Moral presumption functions like "legal presumption" in a court of law. For example, according to legal presumption in the United States, a person accused of crime is presumed to be innocent until he is proved guilty. The accused may be proved guilty, but it is the prosecuting attorney's responsibility to bear the burden of proof. The defendant need only show that the state has not made its case. If there is any doubt, the defendant is acquitted. Similarly, in a discussion of economic inequalities, I have suggested that we ought to assume that they are contrary to Christian ethics until the doubt is removed.

order to compensate for an inequality—as when a golfer must play with a handicap so that he and his competitors will be on even terms. A paraplegic requires much more in the way of expensive treatment and equipment just to become equal in some sense to his fellows. Some people need eyeglasses, others do not. Some limp along through life under a variety of ailments, while others never seem to have a health problem. Some learn quickly in school and like to work on their own. Others may need special tutoring. And so on. The recent adoption of the Medicare program illustrates the principle with respect to the elderly. They obviously have greater need for medical services, on the average, and the program represents an effort to redress a health imbalance. Unfortunately, income distribution often ignores this question of need, with the result that some of those with greatest physical need have the lowest income while some of those with highest income have least need. But, as an exception to the general rule of equality, differences of physical need surely seem a valid reason for some differences of income.

Second, there are inevitable differences in function and responsibility requiring different economic resources for effective service. I am not here speaking of the idea that certain functions ought to be rewarded more handsomely than others, but rather of the fact that certain functions *require* more material support than others. The head of a family of children obviously has a function and responsibility requiring more material resources than a bachelor. Workers of all sorts have to have the tools of their trade: physicians must have ready access to complicated equipment, lawyers and scholars have need for books and special library facilities, organizational managers have need for a variety of special facilities such as expensive computers and ready access to transportation and communication, and so on. A good case can also be made for special material compensation in view of the unusual demands of certain occupations. The President of the United States, for instance, has recreational needs far in excess of those of average persons who do not have to live with the unusual strains of that office while imprisoned in the White House. Mass, complex society creates certain functions which, in turn, require differing degrees and kinds of material resources.

Third, patterns of consumption are affected by differences of

96

inclination, cultural taste, and age. The books which are highly prized by the scholar might be viewed with amusement by the outdoorsman, and the mountain climber's equipment might be totally useless to the musician. If we mean anything by individual integrity and creativity, we cannot reduce persons to a sameness in their patterns of consumption. And if mutuality of experience is to be meaningful, people must be free to create and share different kinds of treasures with one another. Of course this does not necessarily justify large differences in patterns of private consumption, so that some people have the resources to cultivate exotic interests while others are culturally deprived. It does simply suggest that some will use their resources differently than others and that income needs may therefore vary.

Fourth, there is the difficult question of incentives. Equality of income would almost necessarily do away with an economic form of incentive. What would happen to the economy without this form of stimulus? Would production be greatly reduced? If so, a strong case can be made for inequalities of income as a necessary byproduct of the use of incentives to stimulate production. As economists are fond of reminding us, it is not just a question of how the pie should be divided. We must also concern ourselves with the size of the pie. There would seem to be little moral gain in a state of grinding poverty in which all were equally deprived if the introduction of some inequality via incentives would so enlarge the total economic pie that everybody would have a larger slice. The inequality might be harmful in some of its effects upon community life, but it would be a "lesser evil" than that of total poverty. Thus, the inequality would be able to bear the burden of proof.

The validity of this point hinges on the actual effect of incentives on production. There is indeed much evidence to support the view that production is importantly related to economic incentives. On the level of common sense, most of us are aware of things we have done and decisions we have made on the basis of economic gain. As a special kind of evidence, we are also occasionally reminded of the agricultural experience of socialist countries, such as China and the U.S.S.R. When such countries have attempted to collectivize farming, this has apparently slowed production down sharply. Collectivized peasants, producing for a

97

remote urban market without any extra reward for increased productivity, have not done as well as peasants farming their own plots of land. Both the U.S.S.R. and China have had to retreat from collective farming experiments, at least to the extent of permitting peasants to have small gardens and a few animals on the side. When American industries have employed special incentive schemes (including time-and-a-half for overtime), this has doubtless contributed to greater effort and productivity. And many people in the small business field (small shops, service stations, and the like) are doubtless motivated to spend much longer hours in their work because the result of their labor will be theirs to keep.

But before we leap too quickly to justify inequalities of income on the basis of incentives, we ought to remember that there are competent observers who do believe that cybernation will largely make traditional incentives obsolete. Some enthusiasts probably overstate the case. But individual *effort* by individual workers is, indeed, becoming less important in a number of fields of production. Interestingly, American agriculture is moving in the opposite direction from land reform schemes to involve individual farmers in the cultivation of their own plots of land. Huge corporation farms have taken over many thousands of acres from the single-family farms, and the increased efficiency has expanded production. Anyone desiring to justify incentive inequalities on the basis of production needs should be prepared to show in concrete terms how such incentives are essential in modern technological production.

Moreover, if incentives are necessary, we must not forget that there are noneconomic forms of incentive. Social recognition is an important one. As a matter of fact, it may be that the so-called economic incentives are important to many people for social rather than economic reasons. A salary raise may be more important as a symbol of approval than as increased purchasing power. When multimillionaires like Nelson Rockefeller and John F. Kennedy provide public leadership at great personal sacrifice, the incentive can scarcely be an economic one! As we have already noted, studies show that the real motivations of top business executives may not be primarily economic at all. Pure altruism alone may be an inadequate incentive for society to rely upon in view of the amount of human selfishness and inertia. But there may be noneconomic incentives which are less damaging to God's intended covenant community than large inequalities of wealth.

The fifth practical and necessary exception to the rule of equality is based on the difficulties and risks in attempting to change any existing pattern of income distribution. To be sure, the moral presumption must lie with the norm of equality, not with any *status quo*. Nevertheless, the consequences of attempting radical changes too abruptly must be a part of the moral calculation. In some extreme situations, revolutionary social conflict is desirable, but we cannot simply assume that it will be even where disproportions of wealth and income are extreme. One must anticipate the effect of change upon production and upon other social and political structures of the society. In the United States disparities of income and wealth are indefensibly great. The fact that the upper fifth of the population have an average income eight times the size of that of the lowest fifth creates barriers to genuine social interaction which could not possibly be justified on the basis of the first four of these practical and necessary exceptions. Nevertheless, this inherited situation cannot simply be abolished. The disparities are far too deeply rooted in the economic, cultural, social, and political fabric of our society. But recognition of the moral problem of such injustice can force us to keep the pressure on it. Through such measures as guaranteed income and tax reform, we may lay the foundation of more defensible distributions of wealth.

A Note on the Moral Birthright of the Young

Many of the themes we have been discussing need to be seen more directly in terms of children. The moral logic of economic equality can be understood most easily here. Most of the economic rhetoric of our society is irrelevant to the young. Our inherited individualistic economic ethic may indeed be most vulnerable at exactly this point. The effect of the "Protestant ethic" has been to make the young hostages for the presumed immoral and shiftless behavior of their parents. This is difficult to defend, even in those cases where the fathers of the young fully justify the attitude. In other cases, where the parents are poor through exploitation or luckless circumstance (including their own upbringing), the

99

fate of the children is even more distressing. In either case, the children are innocent victims. At least at birth all children are morally equal, even by the most heartless definition of those who have given up on their parents. They are not responsible for their own birth, and it is still a bit early to hold them responsible for their own behavior.

This is not an abstract problem. Depending upon where one draws the line, there are about 15 million poor children in the United States (out of about 70 million). In his valuable study of these children and their family situations, Alvin Schorr has documented two important facts which cannot be evaded in a discussion of the ethics of income distribution.[7] First is the fact that poverty level income undermines both the physical health and the social opportunity of children. Since income sets limits to nutrition, medical care, clothing, housing, and cultural opportunities, this fact should not be surprising. Second is the fact that poverty is self-perpetuating. In an illuminating study of the family cycle of poverty in the United States, Schorr demonstrates the interrelationships among low income, low educational achievement (and school dropout), early marriage, low occupational aspiration, and family breakdown. These interrelationships create a vicious circle strongly predisposing poor children to continue in poverty and to pass their poverty on to their own children. Therefore, "most people who die poor were born poor."[8] Significantly, in 1963, 63 percent of poor children belonged to families headed by women or to families with five or more children (or both). Such children cannot be helped appreciably by general upturns in the economy. They belong to what Schorr calls "poverty-vulnerable families." Obviously the economy is not providing for their personal fulfillment and for their opportunity to participate in the life of human community. And yet it is difficult to cite any ethical reason why they should not have precisely the same opportunity as every other child.

Present Aid to Dependent Children programs of the federal and state governments are based upon the moral claim of the young. While there might have been considerable political opposition to

[7] *Poor Kids: A Report on Children in Poverty* (New York: Basic Books, 1966).
[8] *Ibid.*, p. 23.

aid for the presumably immoral or undeserving parents, politicians could mount a strong case for aid to the children. But the amounts have rarely been sufficient for the social needs of children, and in many states even the most basic and obvious physical needs have also been neglected. Furthermore, eligibility was limited by Congress in 1967 to the proportion of AFDC families on state welfare rolls as of January, 1968, regardless of need, and mothers were required to accept work or work training as a condition of receiving aid. Such measures hardly seem to take seriously the moral claim of the children.

Roman Catholic moral teaching has attempted to deal with the income problem of families in an interesting way. According to Pope Leo XIII and subsequent Catholic authorities, a "just wage" is an income sufficient to provide for the physical and social needs of *families*. It is not based simply upon what the wage-earner has produced. Nevertheless, Catholic teaching is somewhat equivocal at this point. The family basis of income is based upon "social justice." At the same time, it is recognized that wages need to be based upon what the work is worth to the employer—this is commutative justice. The employer is taught to observe the social justice standard (based on family need) when he can afford to do so, but if he cannot then he is bound only to the standard of commutative justice.[9]

The two standards in Catholic teaching point to deeper dilemmas. Shall we define income individualistically or in terms of families? Shall we consider children to be the responsibility of their parents alone, or are they to be considered the children of the whole community? Shall children be given a genuine place of equality as a part of their patrimony, or shall it be tacitly assumed that their economic standing should be limited to what their parents are capable of earning? Those who view families as self-sufficient units may not be troubled much by present practices. But those who have a wider view of social solidarity of the whole human family under God will insist that the economy undergird at least equality of opportunity for all children.

[9] See Edwin G. Kaiser, C.PP.S., *Theology of Work* (Westminster, Maryland: The Newman Press, 1966), pp. 282 ff.

A final comment should be made concerning the birth of children in poverty. Some may feel that, while children are not themselves responsible for their condition, society cannot assume responsibility for the failure of parents to practice birth control. Popular imagination even conjures up images of welfare mothers systematically turning out babies each year in order to increase the size of the relief check, despite the fact that in most places additional payments do not even cover the additional expenses caused by new babies. But again, it is not the child's fault. If we neglect the children we undermine the moral basis of our own community. We also invite the perpetuation of social malaise from generation to generation. Encouragement of birth control is one thing. But once a child is actually born, he has the same standing before God as any other person and his well-being and future promise must be protected. Even if society should some day find it necessary to limit population expansion much more directly, the practice of neglecting children who have already been born can make no contribution to that objective.

Private Income vs. Public Income

Thus far we have treated income largely as a personal or family matter. We have assumed that income is what we use for private purchasing power. Indeed, most advocates treat guaranteed income in this way. It is a guarantee of private consumption.

But now we must remind ourselves that income can be public as well as private. When we speak of the moral objectives of an economic policy, we have more than personal life in mind—we are also thinking of the life of community. But for community to exist, there are some things which must be used in common. Adequate attention to public needs may be quite as important in its way as attention to private needs. As a matter of fact, one can privately be very wealthy and still share in communal poverty. A wealthy man, living in one of our large cities, may have to choose between sending his children to miserable public schools or expensive private ones. He may have to spend more than an hour each morning and evening commuting to and from his work in the city, traveling at snail's pace over automobile clogged highways.

The water he drinks and the air he breathes may be polluted. His family may lack swimming facilities, and there may be no place for him to take his wife and children for an afternoon picnic. His city may have poor library and museum facilities, and he may have to travel hundreds of miles to indulge his growing appreciation of drama and music. When he is sick there may be no decent hospital and clinical facilities at hand. On the other hand, a poor man living in another city could have access to excellent facilities at all these points despite his low personal income. His basic health, educational, and recreational needs may be provided despite his low purchasing power.

Apparently we need to be concerned about both private and public income and about private and public property. If we neglect the private aspect, we fail to undergird the personal dignity of individuals, and the result is personal poverty. If we neglect the public aspect, we fail to undergird the communal life, and the result is public poverty.

Experience with public housing may illustrate neglect of private income. Some well-meaning liberals have emphasized the importance of public housing in our great cities. Such housing has, in fact, often been a boon to those fortunate enough to get in. But it has also had a noticeably demoralizing effect upon many people. Since they are somehow living in "public property," surrounded by a host of impersonal regulations and often supervised paternalistically, people living in public housing sometimes cannot feel that they are really in their own homes. It may be difficult to consider this a space which is uniquely theirs. And consequently attitudes toward the upkeep of property and the development of a sense of neighborhood community have suffered. For this reason, some creative leadership is beginning to experiment with rent supplement programs for the poor and with programs designed to make it easier for the poor to own their own homes or apartments, thus giving them a personal stake in the place where they live.

On the other hand, some well-meaning conservatives have taken the view that everything should be private. Milton Friedman has gone so far as to insist that schools and national parks and the post office system all should be in private hands, so that people can choose to pay for the things they wish to use. The ultra-conserva-

103

tive periodical *Christian Economics,* which is deeply suspicious of any governmental activity beyond protecting the lives and property of citizens, calls for private associations to handle all collective problems, including even roads, public health, schools, irrigation, flood control, conservation, parks, recreation, etc. But what a world this would be if the price of everything we used had to be carefully calculated, so that we would not get anything we hadn't paid for! Even the "robber barons" endowed libraries, museums, zoos, and such cultural facilities for free public use, thus allocating wealth they had gained from unrestrained competitive enterprise.

Private income and private property symbolize and support man's personal dignity and freedom; it is the material basis of man's selfhood. Public income and public property symbolize and support the life of the community as a community; it is the material basis of society. We cannot afford to neglect either one.

What Is the Right Balance Between Private and Public?

It is more difficult, however, to say precisely what the balance between public and private income and consumption ought to be. It cannot be set down in rigid terms.

This relationship really ought not to bother us at all in a book of this kind, except for two things. First, it may help to emphasize that guaranteed income does not mean "socialism." Socialism is only vaguely understood by most people, but in this country it has negative connotations which could sidetrack the real issues of guaranteed income. Secondly, we must not forget that the relationship between public and private consumption will greatly affect the amount of income needed in any guaranteed income plan. As commonly proposed, guaranteed income is a *private* approach. It attempts to place purchasing power in individual hands. It assumes that individuals should be free to make their own personal, private choices in spending this income to meet their needs. It is fully consistent with a private enterprise system of production, and it requires the existence of at least a free market in which free choice can be exercised. Presumably, therefore, the more the human needs which are to be met on a basis other than a free market, the less need there will be for private purchasing power.

104

The point may be illustrated with respect to transportation. In some countries, most transportation within and between cities is by public conveyance, and automobiles are a rarity. In the United States, on the other hand, the automobile has become the basic means of transportation. In this country, therefore, realistic provision for man's social needs usually requires enough money to purchase and maintain automobiles. This includes the very poor, who may be in real trouble without a family car. In public conveyance countries, income may be required for bus and train fares, but the amount is likely to be much smaller. Even within the United States, we may contrast New York City with its inexpensive system of rapid transportation, with Los Angeles which has no rapid transit system and where an automobile is a virtual necessity.

Similarly, in education, medicine, and recreation, if one's needs are provided in the public sphere, one does not have to have as much private purchasing power as one does if it is necessary to purchase those needs in the open market. Without public schools and colleges, parents must use part of their income for tuition, and they must set aside considerable sums to complete their children's educations. But where these things are free, they will scarcely affect the family budget. In 1967, when Governor Ronald Reagan attempted to institute tuition charges at state colleges and the University of California, many Americans became aware for the first time that there are wide differences in the practice of the states in higher education. California, with a highly developed system of higher education at low cost, removes a great deal of the pressure on family income. Some other states, where private education predominates at the higher levels, place a correspondingly greater burden on private incomes to gain the same educational objectives.

The same is true in medicine. Low-cost services at public clinics relieve the family budget. But those who opposed the Medicare program when it was first adopted missed the point altogether when they referred to this as a "socialized medicine" program. On the contrary, it was not a scheme to put government in the business of medicine. Rather, it was an effort to give the elderly more private purchasing power for medical purposes. A real socialized

105

medicine program, such as the one in Great Britain, involves government employment of doctors and the abolition of the fee system (although, in England, this does exist side-by-side with a "free market" in medicine).

These illustrations suggest that we shall have to make some decisions regarding the relationship between public and private spheres, and that these decisions will affect the needs of any guaranteed income programs. Such decisions will have to be under continual review, and we shall have to learn from our experiences with varying balances between the public and private spheres.[10] Undoubtedly, however, we need more immediate emphasis today on the public sector. The free market will never be able to cope with such problems as foul air, polluted water, dirty streets, and insufficient playgrounds. There is little evidence that it can handle our full needs in education, medicine, research, and transportation either. And problems of housing, which are especially acute at the present time, will continue to vex us unless government at least acts to stimulate construction and to regulate the planning of urban developments.

[10] Some people will tend to require any public programs to bear the burden of proof. For an example of this thinking, see Henry E. Wallich, "Private vs. Public," in *Harper's Magazine* (October, 1961), pp. 12-25. Besides questioning the efficiency and economy of public programs, Wallich questions their long-run effect upon civil liberties. He does not doubt the need for some public programs, but he is more impressed by the difficulties in such programs which mix economic questions with political factors than he is with the possibilities of public programs. Others, such as John Kenneth Galbraith, believe that we need much more, not less, development of the public sector. See *The Affluent Society* (New York: New American Library, Mentor edition, 1958), pp. 198-211. While Galbraith believes in a balance between the public and the private, he is alarmed by our neglect of the former for the sake of the latter: "This disparity between our flow of private and public goods and services is no matter of subjective judgment. In the years following World War II, the papers of any major city . . . told daily of the shortages and shortcomings in the elementary municipal and metropolitan services. The schools were old and overcrowded. The police force was under strength and underpaid. The parks and playgrounds were insufficient. Streets and empty lots were filthy, and the sanitation staff was underequipped and in need of men. Access to the city by those who work there was uncertain and painful and becoming more so." (Pp. 198-99.) In the nine years since these words were published, such problems have undoubtedly gotten worse rather than better, thus lending force to Galbraith's viewpoint.

106

Christian ethics, as such, cannot supply answers to the technical problems involved in these areas. But it contributes a basic moral perspective, in which we see such problems in terms of their effect upon physical health, personal integrity, and man's life with fellowman in community.

Chapter VI

SOME QUESTIONS FOR
FURTHER REFLECTION

Guaranteed income will not be a panacea for all our problems. It may even create some new ones which will need to be considered and anticipated. The case for guaranteed income is persuasive on both ethical and practical grounds. But we must not discuss it as though it were a substitute for all other social policies.

In this chapter we shall consider some of these additional problems. No attempt will be made here to have the last word. These are problems which should be given considerably more study than this small book can provide. But I believe that such issues ought to be raised for our better understanding of the implications of guaranteed income and as a contribution to further study and discussion.

Guaranteed Income and Present Welfare Programs

It is sometimes claimed that guaranteed income would make it possible for us to dispense with all our present social welfare programs. As we have already seen, Milton Friedman tends to believe this. One of Friedman's principal reasons for supporting the negative income tax is that "it offers a platform from which an effective political attack can be launched on existing undesirable

108

programs." [1] In his various writings he emphasizes that just about *all* existing programs are undesirable. Even Robert Theobald sometimes regards guaranteed income as a substitute for present programs: "An Economic Security Plan would take the place of the present mosaic of measures: Social Security, unemployment compensation and welfare, subsidies to housing, 'stamp plans,' and all the smaller measures designed to provide for particular 'hardship' cases." [2]

Indeed, the most important thing to be said about present welfare programs is that they are not adequate. If they were, there might be no need for guaranteed income. It may be helpful to remind ourselves, therefore, of several points at which present measures fall short:

1. Many persons in need are not eligible for help. In many states, unemployed but able-bodied men are not eligible, even if they are fathers whose families have no other means of support. (This means that a good father may be forced to desert his wife and children for their economic well-being, since they can receive AFDC welfare payments if he is not around.) Residency requirements exclude large numbers of others, although the courts are beginning to question these requirements. Moreover, in the actual implementation of programs, many who might be eligible legally are discouraged in various ways from seeking coverage. Richard Cloward, and other experts in this field, estimate that as many as half of those legally eligible for help are not presently receiving it. And, as we have noted already, the AFDC program will be limited to the proportion of cases on state welfare rolls as of January, 1968.

2. Aid to those who are covered is generally inadequate. In March, 1966, for instance, aid to dependent children averaged only $35.45 per month per recipient. That same month, payments to the blind averaged only $90.91. These are national averages. Some states, such as New York and California, are more generous. But others, such as Mississippi and Alabama, are very much lower.

3. Welfare payments are administered paternalistically and usually carry a certain stigma. Applicants for welfare are required to submit to the most minute case-by-case examination of their

[1] *Proceedings of the National Symposium on Guaranteed Income*, p. 55.
[2] *Free Men and Free Markets*, p. 120.

present resources. Those responsible for administration are often in a position to make arbitrary decisions. Acceptance of aid appears to require one to confess personal inadequacy. The National Association of Social Workers took note of this in a 1964 statement:

We stand for the abolition of the means test in the archaic form in which it is applied in state and local administration of public assistance. The means test—a comprehensive examination of means and resources, applicant by applicant, as a basis for financial assistance to millions of people—nullifies the objectives of guaranteeing to every individual in our society the right to an adequate and certain income, and does violence to basic human values.[3]

4. There are great discrepancies among the states. As noted above, some states are much more generous than others. This puts pressure on the more generous states to enforce more rigid residency requirements, and it means that residents of the other states suffer disproportionately. But poverty needs to be seen as a national, not a local problem. Effective measures must be nationwide in scope.

5. Social caseworkers are often placed in the role of policemen. Good social workers rebel at having to invade homes in the middle of the night to be sure there is no "man in the house." They recognize that their professional services will be much more effective without having to make case-by-case decisions of eligibility. To be effective, they must be trusted, not feared. For this reason, social workers have increasingly supported guaranteed income proposals.[4]

I remarked above that if present welfare measures were adequate there might be no need for guaranteed income. But when we begin to look at the kinds of inadequacies in present programs it is apparent that only some form of guaranteed income can make them adequate.

[3] Quoted by Edward E. Schwartz, "An End to the Means Test," in Robert Theobald, ed., *The Guaranteed Income*, pp. 141-42.

[4] Some of the police-type assumptions of present programs were revealed in the welfare budget of the District of Columbia for 1967. No additional funds were available for support purposes, but provision was made for the hiring of several more inspectors to make sure nobody could cheat!

What, then, could we dispense with if we adopted guaranteed income?

If the plan adopted were an adequate one certain welfare services would no longer be necessary. Inspectors would not be needed beyond those presently used to check the accuracy of income tax returns. Those aspects of social casework which are solely for the purpose of determining eligibility could also be abolished—and this involves a very large percentage of present social casework. OASDI programs (Social Security) could possibly be abolished as such, including both the payment of premiums by employers and employees and the forms of categorical assistance which it now dispenses. We could possibly do away with unemployment insurance, the farm parity program, and a variety of welfare programs presently designed to give money grants to persons in particular categories. Not to be overlooked, either, is the wide variety of private programs which could be terminated, thus releasing energies to be directed to other kinds of social needs. This would include a number of church welfare programs and also a variety of the agency programs related to "red feather" or "community chest" fund drives.

But there are many kinds of welfare services which have little if any direct relationship to personal income maintenance. They are designed to help people in other ways. Guaranteed income would be no substitute for these services. Included here would be the range of family services, such as marriage counseling, training in homemaking and family child care, and planned parenthood. One should also include the indispensable child services, especially those related to the care of orphans and foster home placement services. The blind and handicapped will continue to need rehabilitative services, whether or not for the sake of increasing their earning power. Group work and recreation services (both public and private) will still be needed. Hospitals, nursing homes, homes for the aged will still be needed very largely on a public and publicly subsidized basis. Community organization is a field of social work which commands increasing interest among social workers, and this field seems particularly important today in urban centers. It will be important with or without guaranteed income. Some cities have begun to experiment with legal services for the poor, and unless guaranteed income grants are large enough

111

to include such services in personal budgets, the experiment may need to be expanded. Public health services of all sorts will certainly need to be continued. And we will hardly be able to dispense with mental hospitals and mental health programs. This listing can only suggest the variety of programs for which guaranteed income will be no substitute.

I would not argue for the permanent desirability of these and other public welfare programs. But their continued existence ought to be viewed apart from guaranteed income. They should be terminated only when public needs disappear or when better solutions can be found.

A word or two might be in order now concerning private welfare programs. The Christmas basket and soup kitchen sort of thing can certainly be relegated to the past, along with anything else designed to meet the most basic economic needs. This will become the business of guaranteed income. Religious and other humanitarian groups ought to be grateful that they can be relieved of the suspicion of manipulating the lives of poor people through relief of their basic wants. As a matter of fact, a number of the programs normally associated with the Community Chest or United Givers Fund can be dealt with now in terms of private purchase of services or public financing. Private groups can instead concentrate more in those areas of service where public sponsorship might possibly detract from private creativity.

Consider the possibilities for church groups. Rather than pouring their limited resources into meeting the basic economic and health needs of the aged or the poor, such groups may do well to bring their programs in religious education up to the quality-levels of better public schools. Furthermore, their resources can well be spent in evangelism and imaginative uses of the mass media of communication. Thus, they can better participate in the ongoing community dialogue, where the mutual exchange of religious witness nourishes the common life.[5] Insofar as they are directly engaged in the more traditional welfare areas, church and other private groups might better use their resources as advocates of the poor and as advocates of enlightened public programs of all sorts.

[5] I have dealt with some of these issues more completely in *Protestant Faith and Religious Liberty* (Nashville: Abingdon Press, 1967).

Half a million dollars spent by church groups in support of humane legislation can be expected to accomplish vastly more human good than the same amount put into a single welfare institution. Guaranteed income, by dealing with the more basic needs (and supplemented by the necessary continuing public welfare programs) ought to release the churches to concentrate with greater directness upon their central tasks of communication.

The Effect of Guaranteed Income on Creativity and Work Opportunity

Elsewhere in this volume we have seen the importance of work. We have viewed it in broad terms as man's total creative response. Therefore we have disagreed with those who propose that we simply accept a new leisure in place of the old work ethic as though we could all just sit down and passively enjoy things.

Guaranteed income by no means rules out work. Indeed, a floor of basic economic security beneath one's feet may increase motivation rather than diminish it. Nevertheless, there needs to be much study of the effects of guaranteed income upon patterns of motivation and creative expression and upon the emerging social needs for work opportunity. I do not think we can simply take all this for granted. In small, face-to-face communities human creativity might be expected to blossom forth without planning or social contrivance. But this is not the kind of society we live in. We have to be aware of masses of people in our great cities, caught up in complex social forces which are confusing and demoralizing. Most of those initially affected by guaranteed income may be culturally deprived; some are already in the second and third generations of nonparticipation in the mainstream of American life. Aside from their lack of cultural tools with which to reorient their lives, such people exhibit low self-esteem and lack of self-confidence. At best, many might simply while away their time before television sets. At worst, some might compensate for low feelings of personal adequacy by various kinds of antisocial behavior. These responses would not differ greatly from what we already see in the emerging crisis of the cities. But a guaranteed income floor might provide

113

us with a new opportunity to do something about the lethargy and antisocial activity of many persons of the tragic urban underclass.

We shall miss this opportunity if we think in narrow terms. Simple reliance upon the ability of private business and industry (bolstered by job-training programs and subsidies) to provide jobs for everyone who might need one is to court disillusionment. In the final analysis, business and industry depend upon profits. The number of jobs available in the private sector will always more or less correspond to the requirements of production for the market. If *everybody* wishing work is to be given a job, government must at least become the employer of last resort. Only government possesses the resources and public responsibility to create programs geared to a flexible number of needed jobs rather than to a market demand for specific goods and services. Moreover, such employment programs can be addressed to some of the important public needs.

Economist Leon Keyserling, who favors the guaranteed income, also favors *"immediate* adoption by the federal government of a guaranteed full-employment policy and program, using federal resources to assure employment for all who are able and willing to work, including such training and educational programs as may be required." [6] He favors this full-employment policy both on economic and social-psychological grounds. He believes that such a policy is desirable for the human fulfillment of the unemployed, but that it is also necessary for the sake of full production in dealing with neglected problems:

We have to rebuild our decaying cities, rehouse the one-fifth of our people who live in urban and rural slums; provide modern medical care and full educational opportunity for all at costs within their means; develop our national resources and clean the air and water; sort out the transportation mess; carry a heavy burden of national defense, which may go on for years, with or without the struggle in Vietnam; and try to get to the moon. [7]

[6] Leon H. Keyserling, "Guaranteed Annual Incomes," *The New Republic* (March 18, 1967), pp. 21-22.

[7] *Ibid.*, p. 21.

114

Keyserling argues that "all these goals will require major employment gains during the next quarter century." Such objectives require major participation by private industry, but Keyserling cites them here in order to indicate the need for a governmental policy of full-employment.

To speak of government as employer of last resort really means committing government to hire people to do things which people are not presently being hired to do. Exactly *what* activities might be included is an open question. Education, health, and social work fields can apparently absorb large numbers of assistants and aides so long as specific institutions do not have to pay the bill. These are the services which Seymour Melman has described as the "human care of human beings" which can never be mechanized. Present Teachers' Aide and Foster Grandparents programs suggest possibilities. Conservation services, and even urban beautification and cleanup programs can likewise absorb large numbers of people when properly organized. Washington, D. C. demonstrated this during the summer of 1967 when PRIDE, Inc. was organized. PRIDE was created as a deliberate effort to provide meaningful activity with remuneration to unemployed young people. It was funded by a grant from the U.S. Department of Labor. The thousand young men involved received $1.75 per hour. They were also given wide latitude in organizing the group and its activities themselves. They declared war on the local rat population and worked at cleaning up streets, alleyways, and vacant lots with notable results. This kind of project took imagination, but it suggests what imaginative approaches to the provision of work opportunity can do.

One problem with most job-creating programs in the past (I am thinking specifically of programs like the CCC and WPA of the Depression years) is that the jobs themselves had no apparent future built into them. They were frankly stopgaps. Consequently, those who held such jobs considered them something to be gotten out of as quickly as possible. We all know how uncreative and unfulfilling work is when it is regarded as a temporary expedient with low social value. It needs to be tied into our own personal development. What we are doing today needs to be a contribution to the greater things we shall be able to do tomorrow. And quite apart from our own personal growth,

115

there is the fact that social relationships need to involve recognition of the contributions people are able to make over a period of years.

For such reasons as these, Professor Frank Riessman and others have begun talking about the "new careers" approach to government job programs. Pointing out that a career is different from a "job" in that a career provides permanence, personal development, and upward mobility, Riessman urges the creation of many new kinds of careers which can begin at quite simple levels. To illustrate, he thinks of teacher's aides, social work assistants, and so on as the beginning rungs on professional ladders. Being a teacher's aide could be the first step toward becoming a teacher, particularly if the "in-service training" aspect could be combined with part-time study. Riessman's concept may be similar to the old apprenticeship concept, although he applies it to a whole new range of professions. And he suggests that government funds be used to create the opportunities at the lowest levels of the professions which are to be involved.[8]

Such proposals, which involve government organization and support of a fabric of new opportunities, merit further study and experimentation. But at the same time we should recognize more fully the social value of many things which are already being done. People need to regard many present activities as worth spending a life in doing. Guaranteed income may provide the economic basis, but there has also to be a greater social awareness of the value of some kinds of contributions which are presently taken for granted.

The most important of these is probably the role of the mother. Whether or not there is a husband and father in the house, the mother's role is one of the keystones of our civilization. And yet we still hear people speak of the importance of making "welfare mothers" do something to earn their welfare payments! Congress itself incredibly wrote this insensitive idea into law in 1967 with the provision that welfare mothers could be required to accept work training and jobs as a condition of their eligibility.

---

[8] For the development of his views, see Arthur Pearl and Frank Riessman, *New Careers for the Poor* (New York: Free Press, 1965), and his various articles.

Presumably mothers without husbands do less to earn their living than mothers *with* husbands, although the logic of this is baffling. Even Frank Riessman calls for improved child care facilities to allow "a large number of unmarried women who new spend their time taking care of their own children, to function in meaningful positions if they so desire." [9] Are we to assume that motherhood per se is not meaningful? (Of course, it is doubtless true that mothers without husbands need some release from the sameness of their domestic responsibilities and on this basis might be encouraged to locate other forms of supplementary activity. But this is not the same thing as downgrading the importance of motherhood as a work activity and as a contribution to society.)

Actually, the whole rich fabric of man's communal life is the arena for the social, cultural, and political contributions of every man. Most of the service activities which are presently defined as "voluntary" ought to be seen as work in the perspective of Christian ethics. What would happen to the modern community if suddenly nobody were willing to perform the voluntary service associated with such groups as PTA, Red Cross, Traveler's Aid, service clubs, political parties, League of Women Voters, Boy Scouts, YMCA, etc.? There is no theoretical or technological limit to the number or diversity of such tasks and opportunities. Nor can we draw the line between those who could and those who could not perform them competently. Voluntary activities in a significant church program provide us with a useful model. Generally there is so much happening, and much of it of such obvious importance, that members may find themselves irresistibly drawn into meaningful activity. In a society with guaranteed income, it will be even more important for churches and other voluntary groups to be on the lookout for persons who need more opportunity for meaningful activities.

Theobald's "consentive" idea may have considerable value, too. This is the proposal that persons on guaranteed income be permitted to create things (all the way from craft items or new products to poetry and music) for sale on the open market. Part of the financial return might be retained, with the rest (up to the

[9] "Two Anti-Poverty Strategies: New Careers vs. the Guaranteed Annual Income" (unpublished paper, January, 1967).

amount of the guaranteed income) returning to the public. Theobald believes that new business might emerge in this way. But
the principal merit of the idea is that it could help institutionalize
a way of making one's creative products available to society, thus
also providing a channel for some social recognition. At the
present time it is very difficult for many people to think of making
good things just to give to our fellowmen, but the addition of
a small price tag could add a note of authenticity and seriousness
to what we do. It might be a kind of relative incentive, as
we have been using that term.

To what extent should people be paid for doing the jobs
which are created by government in its full-employment policy?
For reasons which have already been set forth, such a policy
should not be regarded as a *substitute* for guaranteed income.
But would people do this kind of work (including the "new
careers") for "nothing"?

So long as there is inequality of income, and so long as most
people have a connection between their work and their income,
I believe a persuasive case can be made for some pay incentive
for such work, even in addition to the social recognition which
ought to go with it, and even though one is receiving one's
basic support from guaranteed income. The exact percentage
of earnings which one should be permitted to keep before reach-
ing the "break-even" point can be set at any figure. Robert
Theobald has suggested a rather low figure (possibly only 10%)
so that the basic grant can be high. Friedman suggests something
around 50%, but he wishes to keep the basic grant low. Mathematically, a high basic grant and a comparatively low break-even
point would require a low percentage; and in my judgment this
combination is desirable.

This would mean that everybody on guaranteed income would
also be given a guaranteed opportunity to work—and possibly
to begin a new career. He would be able to retain a portion of
his earnings, thus supplementing the basic grant, up to the point
where his earnings exceeded the grant plus the maximum
retainable amount. Then he would automatically leave guaranteed income.

Public policies would have to indicate which kinds of jobs
(or careers) might or might not be included for such remunera-

tion under a work-opportunity program. We cannot go into this further here, but I wish to make a special plea for some inclusion of the work of mothers without husbands. If we really consider their work to be socially useful, it is not logical to exclude them from the additional benefits paid to participants in work-opportunity programs.

What Effect Would Guaranteed Income Have upon Population Growth and Mobility?

Critics of present-day welfare programs sometimes charge welfare recipients with having more children in order to increase the size of allotments. If they happen to live in cities and states with higher payment schedules, such critics also often charge the poor with migrating to their localities in order to receive some of this extra largess. It happens that neither of these charges is borne out by the facts, although both seem logical on the surface.

Nevertheless, both these charges suggest points at which guaranteed income might lead to important social changes. If income were assured and if additional allotments for each child were really adequate for the support of the child, might this not lead to unrestrained population growth? And, if people are guaranteed their basic livelihood, what is to keep them from flocking to the more desirable climate areas (perhaps Florida and California) to live the life pictured in retirement ads?

The first question suggests a possible dilemma. On the one hand, the case for guaranteed income is particularly compelling with respect to children. As innocent bystanders and as future adults they have every right to claim adequate food, shelter, clothing, education, and enrichment. The poor man's son has as great a moral claim upon society as the rich man's. But, on the other hand, if this logic leads to really adequate allotments, the population explosion may get an unexpected and undesirable boost. Of course, if this proved to be a real problem, negative incentives could be built into any given plan. For example, it could be specified that only X number of children would be supported, or that the greater the number of children in each family, the lower the allotment per child. I would greatly regret this kind of measure because the children would suffer, but it

119

would be better than abandoning the guaranteed income concept altogether. It is also possible to establish noneconomic incentives or disincentives, including ordinary forms of social pressure. But before we leap to such solutions, we must remind ourselves that the problem may not exist. Studies in European countries, where family grants were adopted in a deliberate effort to increase the birthrate, show no correlation between these grants and the birthrates. In an article on "Income Maintenance and the Birth Rate," Alvin Schorr concludes as follows:

A rigorous scientific demonstration has not been provided that income maintenance will lead to a higher birth rate or that it will not. A new income-maintenance program would in all probability lead some people, including some people who are poor, to have additional children. But this effect would probably be trivial in relation to concurrent developments and not discernible in subsequent population figures.[10]

In some societies it has actually been demonstrated that attainment of basic economic security tends to put brakes on runaway population growth. This is because it provides a family with economic stability and encouragement to begin planning for the future. Paradoxically, the most insecure families may be encouraged to take a devil-may-care attitude toward everything.

The other question is intriguing. What *would* the effects of an adequate guaranteed income be upon population mobility?[11] Would people go running off to California and Florida? Would they go to the cities, or would they leave the cities? Would they seek to locate themselves close to potential employment, or would they take this as an opportunity to get as far away from temptation to work as possible? Would a new breed of opportunist arise to exploit the new possibilities of relocating families in other regions at considerable profit to themselves?

Nobody can claim to have the answers to such questions. We need to experiment. Corrective social measures can be adopted

[10] In *Social Security Bulletin*, XXVIII (December, 1965), 30. See also an excellent summary of studies of this question in Christopher Green, *Negative Taxes and the Poverty Problem*, pp. 47-48 and 130-37.

[11] For a brief discussion of this neglected question, see William Vogt, "Conservation and the Guaranteed Income," in Robert Theobald, ed., *The Guaranteed Income*, pp. 147-68.

to meet any unusual problems which seem to arise. It may be, however, that patterns of social mobility would be improved rather than worsened. I have in mind in particular the present migration of poor persons from rural areas into crowded urban ghettoes. This migration largely results from the disintegration of the sharecropper system in the south and the further erosion of the small family farm. I believe it would be highly desirable to slow this migration down. The cities can absorb just so many people over a period of time. Undoubtedly one of the important reasons behind the urban riots in recent summers is the large number of poor people whom the cities have not yet "digested." Guaranteed income could help take some of the pressure off. It could even make it easier for some to leave the urban pressure cooker, and it could help shore up the economic life of small towns. It could become the basis of economic renaissance for the rural south and Appalachia. If guaranteed income rates are constant for the entire country (which would also be the easiest way to handle any program), the long-range effect might also be one of stabilizing cost-of-living levels throughout the United States. I do not offer these as conclusions or predictions, but as interesting possibilities.

Would Guaranteed Income Corrupt Responsible Government?

A hundred years ago, John Stuart Mill warned of the danger to democracy should people be in a position to vote themselves public benefits without having at the same time to pay taxes. Mill, who was both a great economist and political philosopher, believed that "those who pay no taxes . . . have every motive to be lavish and none to economize." If they are permitted to vote they will be allowed to "put their hands into other people's pockets for any purpose which they think fit to call a public one." Henry Hazlitt, who reminds us of this passage in Mill's *Representative Government,* likewise urges that relief and welfare recipients not be allowed to vote.[12] He suggests that "all relief be stated in the form of a monetary debt equal to the cash value of the relief; that no relief recipient be eligible to vote as

[12] *Proceedings of the National Symposium on Guaranteed Income,* p. 58.

long as any part of his debt remains outstanding, but immediately eligible to vote again once the debt is repaid." There would thus "cease to be an enormous vested interest in building up the volume and variety of handouts and the number of recipients. As the recipients would not have votes, demagogic politicians could not appeal to these votes; they would have to appeal exclusively to those who were paying the relief or would be expected to pay for it."

When Hazlitt made this proposal to a national gathering of businessmen, he was laughed down. Undoubtedly the businessmen showed good judgment. But the underlying question of the effect of guaranteed income upon democracy is one which must be considered seriously. Would we invite irresponsible attitudes among those who are entirely on the receiving end of public benefits? Would we open the way for demagogic political uses of a large new interest group?

The question cannot be ignored. Healthy democratic government which encourages maximum public dialogue and participation and maximum commitment to the public interest is ethically important.[13] Historically, the major critics of democracy have most frequently charged it with leading to mob rule and a bread-and-circuses atmosphere. Would guaranteed income foster this result?

The question is not being raised solely by opponents of guaranteed income or democratic government. Erich Fromm, who believes in both, warns us of "the danger that a state that nourishes all could become a mother goddess with dictatorial qualities." [14] It could become a totalitarian situation, as pictured in George Orwell's *1984*. Fromm believes that such a danger "can be overcome only by a simultaneous, drastic increase in democratic procedure in all spheres of social activities." The danger will be most acute when people, though provided with income security, are excluded from meaningful participation in society, when they are treated only as passive recipients. This is another reason

[13] I have discussed the ethical significance of democratic government more thoroughly in *Protestant Faith and Religious Liberty*, esp. in Chapter V on "The Responsible State in Protestant Perspective."

[14] "The Psychological Aspects of the Guaranteed Income," in Robert Theobald, ed., *The Guaranteed Income*, p. 191.

why we cannot simply adopt guaranteed income (thus taking care of the poor and our consciences) but ignore other social problems and the need to involve the poor in more meaningful lives. Guaranteed income is necessary, but it is not sufficient. Possibly welfare inspectors and investigators, and others whose tasks would become obsolete, could be redeployed to serve the poor as voter registrants and instructors in democratic political process!

There is another aspect of this question which must not be overlooked. That is the fact that meaningful participation in a democratic society requires certain minimum economic conditions. People have to have economic ground to stand upon before they can act responsibly. Moreover, wide disparities of wealth and income may be much more damaging to democracy than the existence of large numbers of people whose basic income is derived from public sources. The most corrupt period in American political history may have been the era of unrestrained laissez-faire capitalism when the tycoons manipulated state legislatures, and even Congress, almost at will. Large concentrations of wealth can quite readily purchase influence in the political arena. John C. Bennett has commented wisely that "if democracy is not to be undercut by economic institutions, wealth must be widely distributed, there must be many centers of economic power which can keep one another in balance, there must be real opportunity for the people of all classes to develop their capacities, and there must be a fluid class-structure." [15] Guaranteed income ought to contribute greatly to the further redistribution of income and to a narrowing of some of the worst disparities of wealth in this country.

Furthermore, articulate political power for those who depend upon guaranteed income may be useful in itself. If the levels of guaranteed income are basically set by those who are already prosperous, the tendency will be to keep them too low. Some people will oppose any payments at all, and others may resent having to pay taxes to maintain others at a decent standard of living. This attitude would be shortsighted and selfish. But it could be politically powerful, and it would need to be checked.

[15] *Christians and the State* (New York: Scribner's, 1958), p. 159.

Finally, of course, we must not forget that the wealthy and prosperous have been successful, beyond the dreams of the poor, in gaining subsidies and economic benefits from public sources. Subsidies to huge farm interests, depletion allowances for oil interests, technical assistance for telecommunications interests, cost-plus contracts for defense industries, and subsidies for transportation interests suggest that it is not only the poor who know how to use political power to further private gain. Indeed the poor may have some catching up to do! For in the final analysis the vast discrepancies of wealth and income, the juxtaposition of affluence with deprivation, are more likely to corrupt our form of government than any efforts to correct these conditions.

Guaranteed Income in the World Perspective

Perhaps the most difficult moral and practical question of all is the relationship between guaranteed income *within* the United States and the incomparably deeper poverty problems of Asia, Africa, and Latin America. Morally speaking, is it proper to raise the income of the poor in the United States while we are doing so little abroad? A family income of one or two thousand dollars—well below the American poverty line—might place one in the upper middle class of India, where the average annual income is around $70 per person. There are half a billion people in India, most of them desperately poor. This is more than twice the entire population of the United States and perhaps fifteen times the number of people below the poverty line in this country. Add other Asian countries and much of Africa and Latin America to see the full dimensions of the real world poverty problem.

America's sense of responsibility in dealing with world poverty is clearly diminishing. During the period of the Marshall Plan (1948-53), America contributed some 2 percent of its gross national product for the reconstruction of Europe. During the nineteen fifties, the momentum continued for economic development of other areas, but with steadily smaller grants. By 1967 we were providing less than .3 percent of our gross national product for all of Asia, Africa, and Latin America, and most of this was in the form of loans, rather than grants. In dollar amounts, the 1967 foreign aid appropriation bill was the lowest in a generation. The Vietnam war was consuming more American dollars each month than the amount of economic aid to the rest of the world for the entire year.

A statement by the Council for Christian Social Action of the United Church of Christ (adopted January 30, 1967) summarized the moral implications well.

The poverty of two-thirds of the human family is the starkest economic fact of our time. It is more than a material condition: it is a moral outrage. The sufferings and the degradation of the poor have been made intolerable in our generation. The nations together now possess the technological capacity to lift the burden of poverty from the backs of every people. . . . Our very affluence tends to muffle the cries of human need and to stifle our response to them.

Barbara Ward, who has suggested that the affluent nations "tax" themselves one percent of their gross national products each year for foreign aid, confronts us with the fact that social justice at home is not enough if there is misery abroad. We can usefully ponder her words.

I would have thought that the gap bettween rich and poor must become one of the clearest responsibilities of the ecumenical movement. The fact that our world is so constituted as to create an immense concentration of wealth in our own group . . . and immense concentrations of misery elsewhere compels us to ask ourselves whether it is enough to accept the precepts of social justice simply for our own national tribal, parochial, inward-looking group. Does our justice stop at frontiers? Do our obligations, supported by a wealth derived from worldwide sources, cease at boundaries written not by nature but by history on arbitrary maps? This is the fundamental question. Do we worship a tribal God? [16]

This is the moral question. Can we create a prosperity ghetto, or even a justice ghetto, in the midst of such a world?

[16] "A Challenge to Affluent Nations," in Andrew W. Cordier and Kenneth Maxwell, eds., *Paths to World Order* (New York: Columbia University Press, 1967), p. 100.

To raise this issue is necessarily to mark our work as incomplete, for it is infinitely easier to see and define the problem of guaranteed income within the context of one prosperous nation than it is in world perspective. Facile attempts to gloss over this problem will not help us. To say that Americans have more energetically conquered their environment, and thus have earned full rights to the resulting prosperity, raises the same moral questions of "earning" and "deserving" which we have already discussed. Moreover, it neglects the fact that our society was uniquely favored in the economic resources it inherited in the sparsely inhabited North American continent. It also quite overlooks the bountiful resources we every day receive from the far corners of the world, largely as a result of favorable trade relationships.

It may also be a bit too facile to speak, as Robert Theobald has done, of the social development which must precede economic development in the underdeveloped lands. In *Free Men and Free Markets* Theobald suggests that the real "barriers to change throughout the world are not primarily economic but social and cultural." He did not believe that the poor countries could effectively use more than 10 to 20 percent of the yearly increases of the rich countries' production, even if the rich countries were willing to give the maximum. Real scarcity, he argues, "has been abolished on a worldwide basis. The barriers to change throughout the world are not primarily economic but social and cultural." [17] While there is much truth in such views, they too easily help us rationalize selfish complacency. Furthermore, such a viewpoint may neglect the massive capital needs for such things as hydroelectric power, highways, railroads, and port facilities. It may also make us complacent about the role which the more developed nations can play in the social and cultural fields.

Should we therefore de-emphasize guaranteed income while addressing the more burdensome problems of world economic development?

There are at least four reasons why we should not further postpone guaranteed income in order to deal solely with the needs of the underdeveloped countries, urgent as these needs are.

[17] *Free Men and Free Markets*, p. 150.

In the first place, we need to remember that relative poverty is morally significant. Even if one is not starving to death, he may suffer serious social deprivation. Provided one's basic survival needs are met, it is humanly better to be poor among equals than to be only moderately poor among the wealthy. Measured in absolute terms, the middle class of the nineteenth century lacked many of the things which poor Americans today take for granted. But they did not have to wear a badge of inferiority among their fellows, and this is more important. In balancing the moral claims of the poor of other lands and the poor of America, we have to think not only in absolute terms but in terms of their relative standing in their respective society—although we need constantly to remember that the basic survival needs of many of the world's poor are not being met and that the absolute needs of the American poor are greater than many people suppose.

A second reason for not postponing guaranteed income is that the will of the American people to deal with poverty abroad can be undermined by lack of sensitivity to poverty at home. The more justly economic income is distributed at home, the more likelihood there may be that we can be led to greater sensitivity in our relationships with others. I do not wish to press this argument too hard. I realize that justice within a society can exist alongside complacency toward the suffering of outsiders. Nevertheless, justice within a society may be an important precondition of that society's sensitivity to the needs of others.

A third reason is the fact that we need to be a better model for others to copy. The greater the equality in our society, the more pressure can be placed upon other countries to develop with greater equality. In many countries of the underdeveloped world there is a vast discrepancy between the economic status of a small aristocracy and masses of impoverished people. This is one of the main reasons for the revolutionary mood sweeping through such countries. It would be helpful if those who are struggling for greater justice in such countries could identify more fully with the social achievements of the United States.

The fourth reason is that the political feasibility of foreign aid may be higher if basic needs have been met in a developed country such as the United States. A Congressman may find it

127

difficult to support foreign aid in the knowledge that part of his constituency is in real need.

In any event, we must not let the burden of our international obligations fall upon the backs of the poor. The achievement of guaranteed income in America will not destroy our ability to do many times what we are presently doing abroad. Recalling some of the figures used in the first chapter, it would be possible for us to enact a substantial guaranteed income program and at the same time to double or triple our foreign aid giving—both out of next year's probable increase in our gross national product. We should be doing more, even, than this.

How Large Should Guaranteed Income Be?

We have already surveyed ethical problems which may help to determine the size and scope of the guaranteed income program. I have suggested that equality is a norm, against which deviations ought to be measured (recognizing that there certainly need to be some such deviations). But this norm surely means that guaranteed income should be higher than most advocates are presently suggesting. It should be at least high enough to guarantee full participation in American society. Specific figures should be determined after careful study.

Without attempting to settle the issue, there is one suggestion which can be advanced for further discussion. That is that instead of setting guaranteed income at a particular dollar level, we think in terms of proportionate shares of national productivity. A convenient way to work this out would be to arrive at some percentage of the annual Gross National Product divided by the number of people in the population. The present Gross National Product is around $800 billion, and there are about 200 million people in the country. Dividing 200 million into 800 billion yields $4,000 as the average person's "share" of the Gross National Product. Obviously national productivity cannot simply be divided in this way, but we can take this average share of the GNP as the basis for computing the guaranteed income. Suppose it were decided that a head-of-household (or a single person living alone) should receive a 35% "share" and that an

128

appropriate grant for each dependent would be a 20% "share." On this basis at the present time the dollar amount for the head-of-household would be about $1,400 and the dollar amount for each dependent would be about $800. A family of four would receive $3,800 as its share and as the foundation of its economic security. This would be a comparatively modest figure (ethically speaking), but combined with a work opportunity program, it might not be a bad starting point. Of course the percentage figures could be scaled up or down, in any number of possible combinations.

I believe there are two advantages in using percentages of national productivity rather than a fixed dollar amount in setting the size of grants. The first advantage is that this will always keep the grants in line with actual productivity. If production goes up, so will the grants. If there is a recession and production goes down, so also will the grants. The second advantage is that such a plan would also be a control on the population factor. If the population increases, without corresponding increases in production, then the size of grants will go down (because the total GNP will have been divided into smaller average units). Size of grants, thus, will reflect both the actual productivity of society and the actual size of the population. The setting of grants will not have to be subject to annual political struggles.

Chapter VII

PROSPECTS AND POSSIBILITIES

In one of his poems, Coleridge writes that "work without Hope draws nectar in a sieve, and Hope without an object cannot live." It is impossible to get very steamed up over a hopeless cause; we are better directed to put our efforts where they will count. Is guaranteed income a possibility?

Striking new social ideas always seem impossible. They appear impractical because they have not yet been put to the test of practice. We are creatures of habit, and we do not readily change accepted ways of thinking and doing. Proposed social changes thus inevitably encounter much resistance. This is partly good. Resistance forces us to think and act more carefully, and it may save us from unwise ventures. But it can also have the undesirable effect of making good proposals seem impossible and thus destroy our will to act on them.

So far as economic feasibility is concerned, there should be little question about guaranteed income. It is now advocated by an impressive range of economists as one of the best ways to restructure our efforts to meet the needs of the poor. Some are more liberal than others in the size of the grants they propose, but many economists now believe that some income guarantee is now quite practical economically. The vast affluence of our society and the increasing impersonality of its great productive powers both suggest the feasibility of even the most

130

generous of the proposals. And, of course, guaranteed income plans can be tailored to fit practically any economic specification we care to name.

But what about the question of *political* feasibility? Is it a political possibility and, if so, what can be done to support the adoption of an adequate guaranteed income plan? We must now direct our attention to these two questions.

Is It a Political Possibility?

The initial resistances are certainly evident. We have already made note of the Louis Harris poll, taken during the summer of 1967, which showed that 60 percent of the American people were then opposed to the basic concept. Such polls tend to fluctuate over a period of time. Nevertheless, it is evident that the *instinctive* reaction has been to resist, rather than support, the idea. Furthermore, at the present writing expensive international military commitments (particularly in Vietnam) have severely blunted national commitment to the whole "war on poverty." Pressure in the 90th Congress has been to restrict Federal spending, not to increase it. It remains to be seen what the possibilities will be in the 91st and 92nd Congresses and following the 1968 Presidential election. But at the present moment, the political climate cannot be described as ideal for the introduction of major new social legislation such as guaranteed income.

It would, however, be a mistake to take this immediate climate too seriously. Situations can change very rapidly in politics. When they do, one must be prepared to take advantage of new shifts in the political climate. It is particularly important to gauge properly the major underlying forces at work in the nation, for in the long run these make the biggest differences. One such force is certainly the deep unrest of American cities. Obviously this is rooted in poverty and hopelessness. This unrest will not just go away of its own accord. It will have to be dealt with by confronting the underlying causes, one of which is the lack of dependable income security. Even despite the huge fiscal deficit in 1967-68, President Johnson felt it necessary to announce that the Federal Government will become the employer of last resort

unless private business is able to respond immediately to the
need for jobs:

I am going to call in the businessmen of America and say one of two
things have to happen: You have to help me go out here and find
jobs for these people, or we are going to have to find jobs in the
government for them and offer every one of them a job. I think that
is one thing that could be done. I think that will have to be done,
as expensive as it is.[1]

The Washington Post editorially commended this statement, but
urged that such an employer-of-last-resort program not be a substitute for the more basic need of guaranteed income—a view with
which I am in agreement. But the President's statement does
illustrate for us the sense of urgency with which any occupant
of the White House will have to view the problems of unemployment and poverty until they are solved in a really basic way.

Another important force is automation and cybernation, which
can be expected to develop at an ever accelerating pace. While
the total number of jobs may not drop significantly in the next
few years, it is very doubtful whether private industry will, in
any natural way, be able to keep up with the job needs of an
ever increasing work force. The problem of unemployment may
become particularly acute with termination of the Vietnam
conflict and a general easing of international tensions. Although
it is conceivable that industry, combined with government as
employer of last resort, might be able to keep pace with the
need, the growth of automation and cybernation and the increase
in American affluence may dramatize ever more sharply the contrast between the incomes of the poor and the affluent—unless
something is done on a national basis to place a realistic floor
beneath everybody's income.

So far as adoption of guaranteed income is concerned, I suppose the most promising political reality is the fact that it is
already being supported by thoughtful people at both the liberal
and conservative ends of the political spectrum. A liberal might
be suspicious of any proposal advanced by a Milton Friedman.
A conservative might question an idea advanced by a James Tobin

[1] *The Washington Post* (December 20, 1967).

or a Robert Theobald. But when it turns out to be the same basic concept, prospects for political success take a new turn indeed. This is the situation we are in. When, in December 1967, President Arjay Miller of the Ford Motor Company gave a very strong endorsement to the negative income tax, he both provided it with significant support and illustrated a growing trend at the same time.

But political gains are rarely made automatically. Significant social reform requires patience and hard work, as Leon Keyserling reminds us in a thoughtful statement.

The issue is neither economic nor financial. It is moral and political. Nor can I accept the view that what we are actually doing now represents the apogee of "political feasibility." The ceiling of feasibility is very much higher than the floor of an easy consensus.

Profound social gains are forged in the heat of battle. This has been our entire history. I believe that the guaranteed annual income in workable form will come to pass in the not-too-distant future, if we steer between the excesses of Dr. Theobald and the limitations of Dr. Friedman, and respond to the common sense and practical idealism of the American People.[2]

It may be that the real danger is that a conservative-liberal consensus on guaranteed income will seek out a least common denominator level which is not sufficient to provide for the basic economic needs of the poor. Something could doubtless be said for this as a beginning strategy, on the theory that more could be done later on after the initial concept had been accepted. But we must not forget that this has not proved to be the case with the Social Security program. Over a period of thirty years, the size of benefits has not even kept pace with the rising cost of living, much less provided a just share of increases in American prosperity.

We ought to face honestly the question whether our society is capable of redistributing income so as to guarantee a larger share for the poor. It is one thing to tidy up the welfare system, to make it universally applicable through guaranteed income, and perhaps even to increase the benefit levels a bit. Conservatives

[2] "Guaranteed Annual Incomes," *The New Republic* (March 18, 1967), p. 23.

and liberals, the affluent and the poor, all can perhaps join in *this* effort. But it may be a different story when it actually comes to reducing the gap between the rich and the poor and truly guaranteeing to all a decent standard of living. Even among those who favor the most radical redistribution of income, there are some who doubt whether the politically powerful privileged classes will permit such change. Seymour Martin Lipset, who is perhaps the leading American political sociologist, asserts that "all privileged classes seek to maintain and *enhance* their advantages against the desire of the underprivileged to reduce them. . . . Ruling strata under *all* economic and social systems will try to institutionalize their superiority so that their kin may inherit." [3] (Lipset makes clear that he is thinking of Russia and China as well as the United States and other countries in this indictment.) In a democracy, we can expect the political power of the disprivileged to check this tendency by the more fortunate to increase their superior status.

But here is where poverty now confronts us with a new kind of political problem. The 30 million poor who would mainly be benefited through guaranteed income generally lack the cultural skills necessary for effective political action. And even if they had them, they are vastly outnumbered by the middle- and upper-class affluent. They can "raise hell" in the cities, as some have done. But it is another question whether they are otherwise politically powerful enough to change the distribution of income in any significant way. By themselves this is doubtful indeed. The majority in American society is powerful enough to put down the disorders of the poor in quite repressive ways and to remain aloof to their human miseries.

In a perceptive analysis of this underlying problem, Michael Harrington notes that there is no major political and social force which seems capable of taking hold of events and steering them toward a more hopeful human destiny.[4] Traditionally, the moving power behind social reform has been the irate masses who have become awakened to the injustice of their plight. One can

[3] *Political Man: The Social Bases of Politics* (Garden City, N. Y.: Doubleday Anchor Edition, 1963 [1960]), p. xxii.
[4] *The Accidental Century* (Baltimore: Penguin Books, Inc., 1965, 1966), pp. 292 ff.

illustrate this with the labor movement, movements for national independence, or the civil rights movement. But today we have a "powerless underclass" and a "somnolent middle class," both of which are immobilized by the vastness of the corporate life of society and by their own increasing cultural decadence. Harrington believes that our problem is "one of finding a political equivalent of poverty" because the dispossessed have in the past performed the function of keeping social injustices and insensitivities on the agenda until solved. Otherwise, all of us may sink deeper into social decadence. Private self-seeking and materialism, and a more rigid social status system, may replace the humane and democratic community which is the basic Western ideal. (Harrington relates the decadence of Western art and literature in the twentieth century to our growing inability to control economic and social life and to direct it toward humane ends. His point might well be pondered when we consider the reasons for the growth of secularism and the increase in social irresponsibility in the contemporary world.)

A Unique Opportunity for Christian Action

At this point we may conclude this small book with a consideration of what can be done by Christians and others who share their basic values. We must confess that Christianity has not been considered a very revolutionary force in the modern world—not by the people who have been most alert to the need for social change. Christians seem to be on all sides of all issues; as if it did not really matter where one stood as a Christian. To make matters worse, the behavior of Christians has so often been more easily understood on the basis of their economic interests than on the basis of their faith in God and their commitment to the family of man. When poor and dispossessed, they have sometimes manned the barricades and picket lines. But with the beginnings of affluence, they have seemed willing enough to say that "godliness is in league with riches." The charge may not be fully justified. But this is the way it has appeared to many people of social conscience who have become alienated from the church.

135

But while many such people have not taken the revolutionary possibilities of the church very seriously, it must not be overlooked that only those whose passion for change transcends their own self-interest are ultimately revolutionary. Only those who seek good for the sake of the good itself can be trusted to keep faith with a social vision *regardless* of its effect upon their economic and social status. On occasion Christians, as Christians, have demonstrated precisely this form of passion for justice. The 1948 Amsterdam Assembly of the World Council of Churches expressed the need in striking language:

We have to learn afresh together to speak boldly in Christ's name both to those in power and to the people, to oppose terror, cruelty and race discrimination, to stand by the outcast, the prisoner and the refugee. We have to make of the Church in every place a voice for those who have no voice, and a home where every man will be at home.

This ideal has been fulfilled by actual Christians in relation to slavery, to migrant workers, to the racially disinherited, and to the urban poor. Is the church one of the really revolutionary forces sought by Harrington and others who despair of a new birth of social justice in a world where even Communists sell out to their selfish personal interests?

The behavior of most of us should make us avoid self-righteous pretension. More often than not, Christians have failed. But where we have failed the demands of history, we have also failed to keep faith with our life as Christians.

In suggesting now that Christians may have some unique contribution to make with respect to the guaranteed income issue, I mean to express confidence in the ultimate power of the Christian faith itself. I am not ready to write off Christian behavior as being determined most basically by selfish economic interests and the desire for superior social status. Recognizing that all of us are to some extent corrupted by self-love, it is still possible to affirm the power of the Christian gospel to transform life. If it is God who intended this world to be a garden and mankind to be a community, we must not concede too much to the disruptive power of human sin.

It is, as we have noted, probable that forces now in motion

will eventuate in *some* form of guaranteed income, possibly in the near future. But the active involvement of large numbers of Christians, along with those who are already interested in the question, could make the decisive difference as to the adequancy of programs actually adopted. If we are not able to make a decisive difference immediately, this should not lead to discouragement. Important social changes often have to simmer for a number of years before breakthroughs occur. Christians ought not to be reluctant to be many years ahead of their time, so far as their social goals are concerned. Nor should this be regarded as "utopian." Even a distant social goal is immediately relevant if it increasingly enlists the support of concerned people.

In strategic terms, we should be aware of three levels of approach:

First, the whole matter of discussion and education. Clearly the concept and its moral basis are not yet well understood. Some people will doubtless continue to reject the idea, but they must be given an opportunity to do so intelligently. Others, we may hope, will respond affirmatively. The national discussion now needs to be pushed in as many ways as our ingenuity suggests to us. I know of no institution in American society which will afford more favorable opportunities for this than the churches and other religious institutions.

Second, the focusing of effective political action. The time will come when the issue is directly before us for decision. At that point an outpouring of Christian support from all parts of the land would make a decisive difference, particularly if brought to a focus by church leaders working with other leaders in Washington.

Third, the consolidating of the new economic security program. Undoubtedly any adequate program of guaranteed income will give rise to unforeseen results which are both good and bad. We can rejoice in the good results, but we must be prepared to help in dealing with any problems which emerge. It would be unthinkable for us to win a political victory, and then rush on to other matters as though man's age-old poverty were now, happily, behind us. Christians cannot forget that economic life is *instrumental;* it concerns the *conditions* of man's life in God's intended covenant community. Even the most ideal economic conditions

137

are only conditions. And so the adoption of better economic arrangements ought to be accompanied by more concerted efforts to use this new situation for the sake of real human community. Churches in particular ought to be ready to reach the new guaranteed income recipients as never before: to encourage them to use their new base of economic security creatively and to incorporate them more truly into the life of the total community.

All three of these levels must engage our attention simultaneously. If we attend sufficiently to the task, we may be surprised at the new possibilities which open before us.

APPENDIX

STATEMENTS ON GUARANTEED INCOME BY RELIGIOUS BODIES

1. *National Council of the Churches of Christ in the U. S. A.*[1]

PREAMBLE

The purpose of this policy statement is to affirm the support of the N.C.C. for the principle of a guaranteed income. Although we are not committed to any particular program or method for achieving this goal, we are strongly convinced that this country can and should assure to all its people incomes adequate to maintain health and human decency.

We have come to this position by somewhat different routes. In the statement which follows we declare our major conclusions; we indicate some of the practical and theological reasons which underlie our position; and we affirm our commitment to work with the communions and others both for implementation of the policy and for further clarification of the reasoning behind it.

The National Council of Churches welcomes the growing interest of governmental and private agencies in proposals for a guaranteed income as a method for meeting human need. The President has appointed a commission of leading Americans to study and report to him on new proposals for guaranteeing income. The Department of Health, Education, and Welfare and the office of Economic Oppor-

[1] Adopted by the General Board of the National Council of Churches, February 22, 1968.

tunity have made studies of the guaranteed income. In February, 1967, the President's Commission on Law Enforcement and the Administration of Justice recommended the intensification of efforts for devising methods of providing minimum family income. The Chamber of Commerce of the United States sponsored a National Symposium on Guaranteed Income where various approaches were examined. The report of the National Commission on Technology, Automation, and Economic Progress recommended to the Congress that it investigate new approaches to the problem of income maintenance. The Ripon Society has supported the concept of a "standard" family income. The Advisory Council on Public Welfare issued a report in June, 1966, advising the establishment of need as a single criterion of eligibility for receiving transfer payments, and supported a national minimum standard for public assistance payments.

RELIGIOUS AND ETHICAL ASSUMPTIONS

In a policy statement entitled *Christian Principles and Assumptions of Economic Life* adopted by the General Board of the National Council of the Churches of Christ in the U.S.A. in 1954, certain fundamental religious and ethical assumptions concerning economic life were set forth:

All the resources of the earth . . . are gifts of God, and every form of ownership or use of such property should be kept under such scrutiny that it may not distort the purpose of God's creation. God is the only absolute owner. Every Christian particularly should look upon all of his possessions, as well as his talents, as a trustee, and should use them in the light of his understanding of God's purpose for him. . . . That the material needs of men be met through their economic institutions and activities is one condition of their spiritual growth. . . . Christians should work for a situation wherein all have access at least to a minimum standard of living. . . . Great contrasts between rich and poor in our society tend to destroy fellowship, to undermine equality of opportunity, and to undercut the political institutions of a responsible society.

CONCERN FOR HUMAN NEED

In an era of national abundance, the unmet economic and social needs of persons and families become increasingly matters of concern to the churches. This concern has been stated by the National Council

140

of Churches on numerous occasions and in relationship to varying social problems:

(1958) The National Council of Churches "wishes to call to the attention of the churches the needs, spiritual and social, as well as economic, of the large numbers of people who must depend on public assistance." (1960) "Adequate support of public services by church members is necessary to insure basic services of sufficient quality and quantity to meet the needs of the whole community." (1960) "Be it resolved that the churches be urged to work for availability of adequate public assistance for all needy people. . . ." (1966) "Although a steady and adequate flow of income to the poor is essential to the elimination of their poverty, the Church must work for the restoration of selfhood and dignity and meaning to the lives of those whose economic poverty has damaged or destroyed these essential elements of an abundant life." (1966) "A society, in which abundance replaces scarcity and social structures are increasingly complex, demands reappraisal of traditional forms and relationships." (1966) "Our burgeoning productivity makes possible, and our Judeo-Christian ethic of justice makes mandatory, the development of economic policies and structures under which all people, regardless of employment status, are assured an adequate livelihood."

NEEDS, RIGHTS, AND OBLIGATIONS

As noted above, the General Board has previously recognized that economic institutions exist to meet the needs of persons in community. The fact that these needs can be met only in the relationship of community established a claim upon the individual to contribute to the well-being of his neighbor as well as of himself. It also establishes a claim upon society to furnish those conditions which enable the individual to fulfill his needs and to discharge his obligations. Basic human needs provide clues to the specific character of these responsibilities and rights. A "human right" is a claim to a condition or facility which a person needs in order to contribute to the social good and to live at his best as a person.

Such rights are grounded in the spiritual and moral relationships into which man was created and in which he lives. Whenever social or economic organization excludes persons from effective participation in the economy, they are entitled to assert their claim to the social and physical conditions necessary for the achievement of human dignity. As these claims are met and rights fulfilled, the opportunity

141

and obligation of the individual for the responsible discharge of his duties to the community are correspondingly increased.

Millions of Americans live under economic conditions which deny to them the satisfaction of their basic needs. This situation is scandalous because it is unnecessary. It is immoral because it curtails the exercise of at least two basic human rights: (1) the right to live at a human standard of decency and (2) the right to participate in the control of the conditions of one's life.

To assure these rights, society must move toward full citizen participation by the powerless. It must provide more adequate services for all its members. It must make available sufficient income for those millions of family and individual consumer units which live below contemporary standards of health and human decency.

WAYS OF DEALING WITH POVERTY

Historically and currently, the major efforts to deal with the problems of poverty include: (1) policies to promote economic growth and increase employment opportunity; (2) measures to increase individual employability and productive capacity; and (3) income transfers such as various public welfare and social insurance programs.

There is need for the continuation, intensification, and improvement of all these efforts. For example, a greatly expanded program for providing meaningful jobs could bring many of the poor above the poverty line and greatly enrich our entire society. Such a program is urgent, both because productive activity enhances human dignity and because there are myriads of tasks that need to be done.

INADEQUACY OF PRESENT PROGRAMS

However, thus far our efforts have not eliminated poverty nor solved the problem of distributive justice. Many of the poor will not be helped by expanded employment. Many heads of households under the poverty line are already employed full time. Innovation has replaced the need for the skills of some. Others are too old, too young, or too ill to work. Still others have the responsibility of caring for children and should not be forced to choose between work and want.

These groups require an input of social services and transfer payments in order to meet their basic needs. The National Council of Churches has called for improved levels of payment in both public welfare and social security systems.

As presently designed and administered, however, the public assistance programs fail to provide the answer and frequently violate the human dignity of the poor. Many of those in need are not covered by any of these programs. In most states, payments even for those covered are inadequate, often grossly so. Recipients commonly lose most or all of any supplementary income they may earn. They are subjected to humiliating tests, which in some cases place a premium on family disruption. The National Council of Churches has supported basic reforms in the public welfare program.

NEED FOR AN IMPROVED SYSTEM OF INCOME ASSURANCE

We, therefore, believe that a more satisfactory system of guaranteeing income is both necessary and morally right. Widely discussed proposals for effecting this policy include the negative income tax, demogrants, family allowances, and improved welfare programs based on need as the single eligibility criterion with adequate standards of assistance.

THE PROBLEM OF INCENTIVE

The charge is often made that a policy of guaranteeing family income would destroy the incentive to work. As noted above, for many of the poor, employment is not a solution. Nevertheless we recognize that motivation must carefully be taken into account by any plan for assurance of income. Many proposed income assurance plans are designed to encourage the earning of additional income, rather than discourage it as some present programs do. Furthermore, motivational research is revealing various sources for incentives besides the economic, such as prestige, power, and social usefulness. Indeed, access to income may strengthen motivation and liberate creativity.

POLICY RECOMMENDATIONS REGARDING GUARANTEED INCOME

In the light of the above consideration, the National Council of Churches endorses the concept and desirability of a guaranteed income. Such a program should meet the following criteria:
  1) It should be available as a matter of right, with need as the sole criterion of eligibility.
  2) It should be adequate to maintain health and human decency.
  3) It should be administered so as to adjust benefits to changes in cost of living.
  4) It should be developed in a manner which will respect the freedom of persons to manage their own lives, increase their power to choose their own careers, and enable them to participate in meeting personal and community needs.

143

5) It should be designed to afford incentive to productive activity.

6) It should be designed in such a way that existing socially desirable programs and values are conserved and enhanced.

We recognize that the guaranteed income is not a substitute for programs of full employment and human resource development. It is not a panacea for all the socio-economic problems encountered by the family and the individual in the course of a life cycle. At the same time, we are compelled to acknowledge that our socio-economic system works imperfectly. It is, therefore, the responsibility of society to devise new institutions which more adequately fulfill basic human rights.

We recommend that the churches (1) study the various methods for guaranteeing every individual and family in need an income capable of supporting human life in dignity and decency; and (2) participate in the development and implementation of those policies and programs which best fulfill the above criteria.

The National Council of Churches commits itself to share in the continuing study, dialogue, and development of programs consistent with these principles.

Voting for adoption—107; Against—1; Abstaining—2

2. The United Methodist Church [2]

GUARANTEED ANNUAL INCOME

Adequate food, clothings, and housing are a necessary ingredient in the developmental process of the individual. In a high-money economy funds are needed to purchase basic commodities and services. But many Americans today live under economic conditions which deny them satisfaction of their basic needs. This situation is scandalous because it is unnecessary due to the economic productivity of our society.

Present programs designed to produce economic growth and to increase employment opportunities have been inadequate to fill the need, as have the various income transfer systems such as public welfare and social insurance programs.

A national program of guaranteed income is not a substitute for a full employment policy. We believe that programs are needed which will develop the maximum productive skills of all citizens. We also

[2] Adopted by the General Conference of The United Methodist Church, May, 1968.

144

believe that wage standards are needed which provide a living wage. It will still be necessary to broaden and improve social welfare services. However, we must acknowledge that our economy functions imperfectly. It becomes the responsibility of society to develop new institutions which more adequately fulfill human rights. As Christians we have the obligations to develop the moral foundation for public policies which provide every family with the minimum income needed to participate as responsible and productive members of society.

We call upon our churches and the General Board and Agencies: (1) to study the various methods for guaranteeing every individual and family an income capable of supporting human life in dignity and decency: and (2) to participate in the development and implementation of those policies and programs which best fulfill the following criteria:

1) Available to all as a matter of right;
2) Adequate to maintain health and human decency;
3) Administered so as to maximize coverage and adjust benefits to changes in cost of living;
4) Developed in a manner which will respect the freedom of persons to manage their own lives, increase their power to choose their own careers, and enable them to participate in meeting personal and community needs;
5) Designed to afford incentive to productive activity;
6) Designed in such a way that existing socially desirable programs and values are conserved and enhanced.

3. Report of the Special Committee on The Church, the Christian, and Work, United Presbyterian Church in the U. S. A.[3] (excerpts)

VOCATION AND MAN'S RIGHT TO ECONOMIC WELL-BEING

The misunderstood Protestant ethic implies that somehow a man's worth is established as he "carries his share" in the market; but the

[3] Report submitted on February 28, 1967, for transmission to the 179th General Assembly (1967). Received by the 179th General Assembly for study. This document has the status solely of a study resource. It is neither a position paper nor a policy statement on economic issues binding the boards and agencies, judicatories, or United Presbyterians to a particular point of view.

idea of covenant establishes the worth of a man, not in his evidence of economic activism, but in his election by God, his being-in-Christ. More concretely, a Christian need not establish his worth. His worth is given, and his vocation is to render praise in the manifold opportunities which are available to him. In the covenant community, a man does not earn his right to be recipient of the covenant promises. These are his by virtue of his existence as an elected man. Therefore, the dilemma of Christian vocation without occupation vanishes, at least in principle, because the vocation of a Christian can certainly be implemented outside the marketplace. Occupation is not the vehicle for proving worth, and not the indispensable means for the glorification of God. If access to the market is blocked or if the market does not need a man's labors, man may witness his concern for community in a myriad of other ways.

Reasoning by analogy, no man's worth is established by exchange value. A man has supreme value by virtue of his existence in the community, apart from and preceding his economic contribution. A man might not have access to an occupation, because of severe economic displacement, decreasing needs of the labor market, his own inability, or even his refusal to work. But the absence of an occupation is not a denial of his value as a person or his right of existence. This value is granted by God, and merely acknowledged by community programs which maintain a level of economic welfare which is conducive to human dignity. Deep within the Christian faith there is an impulse which drives us to consider sympathetically the various contemporary proposals for a socially assured income. The same insight into human value which encouraged welfare programs in the sixteenth-century village kirk and later in towns, cities, and nations now encourages Presbyterians to be creative in their search for new, morally sensitive forms of human equality. Anyone who refuses to enter the national conversation about the socially assured income ought to search his conscience. Protestants seem perennially to be in danger of confusing slogans from an overly individualistic business ideology with the more profound insights of a Christian doctrine of man.

Nor is economic inactivity necessarily the sign that a man has denied his vocation—vocation here understood as responsible involvement in the community. Participation in the community can and often does proceed in ways other than compensated labor, ways that have not customarily been branded as work in marketplace terms. . . . The point is that the doctrine of vocation has a twofold application: it establishes the worth of man regardless of his involvement in compensated labor; and it calls man to responsible involvement in

146

community, an involvement that may or may not include economic employment in the traditional sense. The Reformed tradition does not condone irresponsible idleness, nor does it say that society ought to provide a luxurious support for those who do not care to work. What it does claim is that every man has a right to exist at the level of welfare that a society designates as "being human"; it also claims that every man has an obligation to be involved in the cultivation of humane social environment. The twofold application of the doctrine of vocation does not involve contradictions, only the acknowledgment of the essentially Christian idea that a man has both value and responsibility.

FOCUS ON ISSUES—PROPOSITION FOR DEBATE

1. A great economic debate of the next decade will undoubtedly concern the establishment of a guaranteed annual income. Such a scheme would mean that a man's right to a minimum level of material welfare would not be dependent upon his contribution in the labor market. Does the Christian doctrine of vocation predispose the Church to favor some form of guaranteed income, or at least a more systematic structure of public assistance and social insurance programs? Must not the Church affirm the inherent worth of man, and bridle when the right of man's dignified existence is established in an arbitrary set of means tests, enforced inconsistently among the various states, counties, cities, and towns? The time has come for debate about the scheme that can most adequately meet society's obligation. But, regardless of the particular schemes proposed, Christians ought to speak clearly on behalf of the duty to provide an income base that is dignified—that does not exclude persons from the level of physical welfare which our society calls human.

2. We ought to resist the idea that the technological revolution is an impersonal force, which man can resist or shape only with great effort. Machines are still tools, albeit very efficient ones. We must be careful about policy decisions that are made in the name of administrative or technical efficiency. Justice is not efficiency, but the adjustment of interest to interest and value to value. Some technical possibilities should be resisted, in the interest of working out just compromises on behalf of human needs. Labor is not automatically in the wrong when it occasionally puts its weight against technological innovation, nor is it automatically right. Rather, innovation is the occasion for compromise and wisdom.

3. Any national expression of concern for the unemployed is meaningless so long as families of the unemployed are kept at an economic level well below that which our government calls "impoverished." Welfare programs vary from state to state, but usually they are subminimum. They are often administered inconsistently, sometimes even cruelly. If Christians believe that a man has a right to economic dignity because he is a valuable creation of God, they ought to participate in the current national effort to evaluate and revitalize welfare programs.

4. Persons who advocate a more systematic and generous provision for unemployment welfare are often chastized for their idealism. "Be practical! Giving money to the unemployed destroys their incentive." The criticism is ill-founded. It assumes that poverty spawns incentive, when actually it breeds ignorance and reduced aspiration. It assumes that a man with a measure of economic success will be content, when actually the taste of success whets the appetite. More profoundly, the criticism grows from the theological and sociological heresy that the just society is one where everyone earns his own way. This view ignores the deeply social and mutually dependent character of our lives that are just as real as the individualized dimension.

5. Our economy has not provided jobs for all who are "able, willing, and seeking to work." Because of this, the National Commission on Technology, Automation, and Economic Progress has recommended that the government assume the role of an "employer of last resort." Adoption of this concept would mean that those who could not find work in the private sector would be offered employment in publicly supported programs. Are Christians called to support programs which assure everyone a job, or should the impersonal forces of the marketplace be the determining factor?

148

SUGGESTIONS FOR FURTHER READING

A "Freedom Budget" for All Americans. New York: A. Philip Randolph Institute, 1966.

Clark, Henry. The Christian Case Against Poverty. New York: Association Press, 1965.

de Jouvenel, Bertrand. The Ethics of Redistribution. Cambridge: Cambridge University Press, 1952.

Eckstein, Otto, ed. Studies in the Economics of Income Maintenance. Washington, D. C.: The Brookings Institution, 1966.

Friedman, Milton. Capitalism and Freedom. Chicago: University of Chicago Press, 1962.

Galbraith, John Kenneth. The Affluent Society. Boston: Houghton Mifflin, 1958.

Green, Christopher. Negative Taxes and the Poverty Problem. Washington, D. C.: The Brookings Institution, 1967.

"The Guaranteed Income," articles in American Child (Summer, 1966).

"Guaranteed Income—How?" articles in Social Action (November, 1967).

Hall, Cameron P., ed. Human Values and Advancing Technology. New York: Friendship Press, 1967.

Harrington, Michael. The Accidental Century. New York: The Macmillan Company, 1965; also: Baltimore: Penguin Books, Inc., 1965, 1966.

_____. The Other America: Poverty in the United States. New York: The Macmillan Company, 1962.

Hoyt, Elizabeth E., et al. American Income and Its Use. New York: Harper & Brothers, 1954.

Keyserling, Leon H. "Guaranteed Annual Incomes," *New Republic* (March 18, 1967).

Lampman, Robert J. "Approaches to the Reduction of Poverty," *American Economic Review, Papers and Proceedings* (May, 1965).

_____. "Prognosis for Poverty," National Tax Association, *Proceedings of 57th Annual Conference, Pittsburgh* (September, 1964).

Miller, Haskell M. *Compassion and Community: An Appraisal of the Church's Changing Role in Social Welfare.* New York: Association Press, 1961.

Moynihan, Daniel P. "The Case for a Family Allowance," *The New York Times Magazine* (Feb. 5, 1967).

Muelder, Walter G. *Religion and Economic Responsibility.* New York: Charles Scribner's Sons, 1953.

Myrdal, Gunnar. *Challenge to Affluence.* New York: Random House, 1963.

Nicol, Helen O. "Guaranteed Income Maintenance: Another Look at the Debate," *Welfare in Review* (June-July, 1967).

Obenhaus, Victor. "The Ethics of Income Distribution." New York: National Council of Churches, Committee on Church and Economic Life, mimeographed, 1967.

_____. *Ethics for an Industrial Age: A Christian Inquiry.* New York: Harper & Row, 1965.

Pearl, Arthur, and Riessman, Frank. *New Careers for the Poor.* New York: The Free Press, 1965.

Proceedings of the National Symposium on Guaranteed Income. Washington, D. C.: Chamber of Commerce of the United States, 1966.

Schaller, Lyle E. *The Churches' War on Poverty.* Nashville: Abingdon Press, 1967.

Schorr, Alvin. "Against a Negative Income Tax," *The Public Interest* (Fall, 1966).

_____. *Poor Kids: A Report on Children in Poverty.* New York: Basic Books, 1966.

Seligman, Ben, and Lekachman, Robert, on The Guaranteed Income: Pro and Con, in *Christianity and Crisis* (Jan. 24, 1966).

Speizman, Milton. "Speenhamland, an Experiment in Guaranteed Income," *Social Service Review* (March, 1966).

Theobald, Robert. *Free Men and Free Markets.* Garden City, N. Y.: Doubleday Anchor, 1965, 1963.

_____, ed. *The Guaranteed Income: Next Step in Socioeconomic Evolution?* Garden City, N. Y.: Doubleday, 1966.

_____. "Guaranteed Income: Short and Long-Run Issues," *Guaranteed Annual Income Newsletter* (May-June, 1967).

Tobin, James. "The Case for an Income Guarantee," *The Public Interest* (Summer, 1966).

_____. "Improving the Economic Status of the Negro," *Daedalus* (Fall, 1965).

Vadakin, James. *Family Allowances.* Miami: University of Miami Press, 1959.

INDEX

Numbers in italic indicate references to footnotes

153